Vertretungsstunden
Englisch Sek I

Bettina Eisermann

Vertretungsstunden Englisch Sek I

Ernst Klett Sprachen
Stuttgart

1. Auflage   1 ¹³ ¹² ¹¹ | 2027 26 25 24

Nachfolger von 978- 3-12-927917-5
Die letzte Zahl bezeichnet das Jahr des Druckes. Das Werk und seine Teile sind urheberrechtlich geschützt. Jede Nutzung in anderen als den gesetzlich zugelassenen Fällen bedarf der vorherigen schriftlichen Einwilligung des Verlags.
Die in diesem Werk angegeben Links wurden von der Redaktion sorgfältig geprüft, wohl wissend, dass sie sich ändern können. Die Redaktion erklärt hiermit ausdrücklich, dass zum Zeitpunkt der Linksetzung keine illegalen Inhalte auf den zu verlinkenden Seiten erkennbar waren. Auf die aktuelle und zukünftige Gestaltung, die Inhalte oder die Urheberschaft der verlinkten Seiten hat die Redaktion keinerlei Einfluss. Deshalb distanziert sie sich hiermit ausdrücklich von allen Inhalten aller verlinkten Seiten, die nach der Linksetzung verändert wurden. Diese Erklärung gilt für alle in diesem Werk aufgeführten Links.

© Ernst Klett Sprachen GmbH, Rotebühlstraße 77, 70178 Stuttgart, 2012. Alle Rechte vorbehalten.
Die Nutzung der Inhalte für Text- und Data-Mining ist ausdrücklich vorbehalten und daher untersagt.
www.klett-sprachen.de

Redaktion: Gabriele Uplawski, Redaktionsbüro, Hannover
Ansprechpartner Redaktion: Wolfgang Volz
Layoutkonzeption: Elmar Feuerbach
Illustrationen: Oliver Lucht, Pfeffer und Salz Kommunikation Freiburg
Gestaltung und Satz: Nena Dietz, Glückssachen Stuttgart
Umschlaggestaltung: Sandra Vrabec
Druck und Bindung: Digitaldruck Tebben GmbH, Biessenhofen

Printed in Germany
ISBN 978-3-12-927927-4

Inhaltsverzeichnis

Vorwort 7

Klasse 5/6

WS 1   The four seasons 8
WS 2   All kinds of animals 9
WS 3   A pet mouse 10
WS 4   My favourite animal 11
WS 5   Animal fun 12
WS 6   How healthy do you eat? 13
WS 7   Making plans for the weekend 14
WS 8   Let's talk: Meeting a friend 16
WS 9   Let's talk: Meeting friends 17
WS 10 Let's read: Three students 18
WS 11 Let's read: Strange neighbours 19
WS 12 Opposites – adjectives 20
WS 13 Opposites – Pictionary 21
WS 14 A crossword (relative clauses) 22
WS 15 Dictionary skills: Alphabetical order 23
WS 16 Verbs, verbs, verbs 24
WS 17 Irregular verbs – a maze 26
WS 18 Irregular verbs – Once upon a time 27

Klasse 7/8

WS 19 Feelings and moods 28
WS 20 Your 'Mood-o-Meter' 29
WS 21 Your eating habits 30
WS 22 Jamie Oliver: 'Feed Me Better' 31
WS 23 A map of Scotland 33
WS 24 Group puzzle: Very Scottish 34
WS 25 Group puzzle: Blackfeet Nation 35

WS 26 Crazy sports 37
WS 27 Let's talk: A bike trip 38
WS 28 In other words 41
WS 29 Adjectives and their opposites 42
WS 30 Jeopardy game: All about adjectives 43
WS 31 Dictionary skills: Look it up! 45
WS 32 Dictionary skills: Finding words quickly ... 46
WS 33 Dictionary skills: A bike 47

Klasse 9/10

WS 34 An Australia quiz 48
WS 35 An Australian bike challenge 49
WS 36 Virtual water 51
WS 37 Spice it up! 52
WS 38 Being polite 54
WS 39 Let's talk: On a class trip 55
WS 40 Food words – a guessing game 60
WS 41 Sport words – a guessing game 61
WS 42 Jobtivity 62
WS 43 Dictionary skills: False friends 65
WS 44 Dictionary skills: Synonyms 66

Kommentar mit Lösungen

Klasse 5/6 69
Klasse 7/8 79
Klasse 9/10 88
Bildquellen 95

Vorwort

Vertretungsstunden lassen sich nicht einplanen, der Lernstand der Klasse ist nicht bekannt und Rücksprache mit der Kollegin/dem Kollegen kann oft nicht gehalten werden. Um in derartigen Situationen stressfrei agieren zu können, wurde diese Sammlung von lehrwerkunabhängigen Arbeitsblättern für den Englischunterricht der Sekundarstufe 1 zusammengestellt. Die Worksheets sind mit wenig Vorbereitung schnell einsetzbar und bieten den Schülerinnen und Schülern eine sinnvolle Beschäftigung mit der Fremdsprache.

Vertretungsstunden Englisch Sek I – das sind realistische Unterrichtsideen für Vertretungsstunden, die lehrplankonform Lebenswelt und Interessen der Schülerinnen und Schüler aufgreifen.

Die Worksheets sind themen- und kompetenzorientiert für die Klassenstufen 5/6, 7/8 und 9/10 und enthalten Aufgaben verschiedenster Art: Lesetexte, Spiele, Wortschatz- und Wörterbucharbeit, Rollenspiele, kreative Schreibaufgaben.
So können auch Vertretungsstunden gewinnbringend sein. Es gibt Worksheets für Einzel-, Partner- und Gruppenarbeit.

Einige Worksheets enthalten Extra-Aufgaben, die sich zur Differenzierung sowohl nach Lernniveau als auch nach Lernertypen eignen. So kann die spezifische Klassensituation berücksichtigt werden.

Klassische Verfahren der Unterrichtsgestaltung stehen neben Formen des kooperativen Lernens. Konzentrationsfördernde Elemente (wie z. B. Abschreiben aus dem Gedächtnis, *Leserätsel in Form von Denksport-Aufgaben*) wurden eingebaut. Spiele sind besonders wichtig, da hier neben sprachlichen Kompetenzen, die eher unbewusst trainiert werden, auch soziale Kompetenzen eine große Rolle spielen. Doch leider gehen Spiele im Unterrichtsalltag aufgrund von Zeitmangel meist unter. Hier bieten gerade Vertretungsstunden die Gelegenheit, dies nachzuholen und den Schülerinnen und Schülern einen Motivationsschub für den regulären Englischunterricht zu geben.

Die Worksheets lassen sich nicht nur in Vertretungsstunden, sondern auch zu einer abwechslungsreichen Stundengestaltung im Unterrichtsalltag einsetzen.

Im Lehrerteil finden sich Kommentare zu den einzelnen Worksheets, Lösungen bzw. Lösungsvorschläge sowie Hinweise zu den weiterführenden Extra-Aufgaben.

Bettina Eisermann

👥	Partnerarbeit
👥👥	Gruppenarbeit
📖	Wörterbucharbeit
WS	Worksheet
SuS	Schülerinnen und Schüler
LuL	Lehrerinnen und Lehrer

Klasse 5/6   Klasse 7/8   Klasse 9/10

The four seasons

1. The seasons of the year

Look at the pictures and fill in the right season.

spring – summer – autumn – winter

....

2. There is a season for everything

All these words have something to do with the four seasons. Work in four groups, one for each season. Copy the table into your exercise book. Then write the words that go with your season in the right list. Use a dictionary, if you don't know the word.

cycling – boots – hot – woollen hat – wearing costumes – pullover – sunny – fleece – foggy – jacket – T-shirt – shorts – playing football – bikini – rain jacket – mittens – trousers – freezing – picking mushrooms – long-sleeved shirt – ice-skating – anorak – blouse – coat – windy – dress – playing inside – skirt – cardigan – skiing – sweatshirt – building a snowman – throwing snowballs – trainers – snowboarding – scarf – swimming – running – sandals – flying a kite – playing volleyball – chilly – playing outside – wellingtons – sun bathing – picking berries – tank top – rainy – short-sleeved shirt – stormy – cap – cloudy – cold – hiking – warm – going sledging

season:		
weather	clothes	activities

3. What's your favourite season?

Read the two acrostics. Then write your own acrostic or a short poem. Decorate the page.

```
    W ONDERFUL
T   I ME
S   N OW
OU  T SIDE
F   E ELS
G   R EAT
```

```
LE    A VES
COLO  U RFUL
KI    T ES
      U MBRELLAS
STOR  M Y
WI    N DS
```

OR: *Write a short story, for example:*

I'm Mike, a tiny mouse. I live outside all year and of course I have a favourite season: autumn. I can go over the fields and pick up food: grain and corn, berries and mushrooms, apples and pears. I like foggy mornings …

All kinds of animals

1. Ten animals

Think of ten animals. Write them down.

....

....

....

....

....

Try to make a word snake.

....

....

....

....

elephant – tiger – rhinoceros – s...

2. Different kinds of animals

Write the animals from exercise 1 into the table below. Add more animals. You can work with a partner, too.

water	wild	farm	pets	birds

EXTRA

A. Make an alphabet of wild animals. Start with **A:** *ape,* **B:** *baboon,* **C:** ...

B. Play the 10-question game with a partner. Think of an animal. Your partner can only ask yes/no questions to find out what animal you are thinking of. Example: Do you live in the jungle? – Yes, I do. / No, I don't.

C. Make an animal wordsearch for a partner. Hide six words in a square of letters.

D. Make an animal quiz with missing letters for a partner. For example: Write down the consonants of the word only, write a line for the missing vowel. c ☐ w

1. Are you looking for a pet?

First read the text. The words at the bottom of the page can help you.

A mouse is a nice pet. It's not expensive and it doesn't need a lot of space. You shouldn't keep only one mouse, two or three mice are better, because they need friends. It's best to keep two mouse girls together.
Mice don't smell, they often clean themselves or each other.
Mouse housing is very simple, a small cage with a wooden box is perfect. Make sure that the mice get enough air to breathe. Place newspapers on the ground of the cage, this makes it warmer. Sprinkle a lot of saw dust in it to soak up the urine. Put a lot of hay in their sleeping area for them to snuggle up in. Clean the cage at least once a week.
Mice love to play, so be sure to place empty toilet rolls or eggs cartons in their play areas, not only to chew on, but to toss around and run through.
Mice also like to run on wheels, it is fun and gives them a lot of exercise. Mice are awake when you are asleep.
Feeding mice is simple. Seeds, a little hamster food, dried bread, grain is all they need. And remember to give them fresh drinking water every day.
A pet mouse can live for about 2–3 years.

a) True or false? Write **T** for true or **F** for false behind the statements. Correct the false ones.

1. A mouse is an expensive animal. ☐
2. A mouse likes to live alone. ☐
3. Don't keep mouse boys and mouse girls together. ☐
4. A mouse needs a cage. ☐
5. Mice clean the cage themselves. ☐
6. Mice need toys. ☐
7. Mice play during the day. ☐
8. It's easy to feed mice. ☐

b) Read the text again. What is good about keeping mice and what is bad?

good ☺	bad ☹

Would you like to have mice as pets? Why or why not?

....

....

space *Raum, Platz* – **housing** *Haltung, Unterbringung* – **cage** *Käfig* – **saw dust** *Sägespäne* – **to soak up** *aufsaugen* – **to snuggle up** *zusammenkuscheln* – **to chew** *on kauen* – **to toss around** *herumschleudern* – **exercise** *Bewegung* – **grain** *Getreide*

1. My favourite animal

Write about your favourite animal. Use the questions to make some notes first.

- What is your favourite animal? ....
- Where does it live? ....
- What does it eat? ....
- What are its enemies? ....
- What is special about it? ....
- Why do you like it? ....

Design a page for your folder. Look at the examples for help.

My favourite animal is the polar bear. It lives in the Arctic regions. It's one of the largest animals on earth. It eats seals. The polar bear hasn't got natural enemies. The only enemies are humans. Polar bears are predators. Every spring they have one or two babies, who live with the mother bear. I like polar bears because of their strength.

I like penguins very much. They live in the Antarctic ice together with lots of other penguins. They are never alone. I like their black and white colour and their special way of walking. The fathers take care of the little penguin babies while the mothers go and look for something to eat for them. They eat small fish.

EXTRA

A. *What is your favourite animal film? Write a text about it. You can use these phrases:*

My favourite animal film is …
It is about …
I think the best part is when …
I like it because …

B. *Write a story with the title "A day in the life of … (your favourite animal)".*

---

enemy *Feind* – **special** *besonders* – **polar bear** *Eisbär* – **human** *Mensch* – **seal** *Seehund* – **predator** *Raubtier* – **strength** *Kraft*

Do you understand the joke?

Here are some animal jokes. Match the questions with the answers.
The words at the bottom of the page can help you. Draw lines.

Question

1. What animal never tells the truth?
2. Why did the grizzly bear catch a cold?
3. Why did it take the elephant so long to get on the airplane?
4. Why did the frog say "meow"?
5. Where should you never take a dog?
6. How do cats buy things?
7. What did the bee say to the flower?
8. Why are dogs such bad dancers?
9. Why does everyone love cats?
10. What kind of pets lie around the house?
11. How do you start a teddy bear race?
12. What's grey and goes round and round?
13. What do you call an elephant that flies?

Answer

a. Because he had to check in his trunk.
b. To the flea market.
c. A lion.
d. Because he went outside on his bare feet.
e. He was learning a foreign language.
f. Because they have two left feet.
g. Carpets!
h. From a catalogue!
i. Hello honey!
j. An elephant in a washing machine!
k. A jumbo jet.
l. Because they are purr-fect!
m. Ready, teddy, go!

EXTRA

A. Draw pictures for some of the jokes.

B. Do you know any other animal jokes? Tell the class.

---

to tell the truth *die Wahrheit sagen* – **to lie** *lügen* – **trunk** *Rüssel; großer Koffer* – **to catch a cold** *sich eine Erkältung einfangen* –
flea *Floh* – **frog** *Frosch* – **meow** *miau* – **bare** *nackt, barefoot barfuß* – **foreign language** *Fremdsprache* – **bee** *Biene* – **carpet** *Teppich* –
honey *Honig, Liebling* – **to lie around** *herumliegen* – **to purr** *schnurren* – **carpet** *Teppich* – **Ready, steady, go!** *Auf die Plätze, fertig, los!*

1. Do you know these fruits and vegetables?

The vowels (a, e, i, o, u) are missing. Can you add them to get the words?

c☐c☐mb☐r   ☐r☐ng☐s   str☐wb☐rr☐☐s

t☐m☐t☐☐s   ch☐rr☐☐s   l☐tt☐c☐

2. Find someone who …

Walk around in class and ask your classmates about the things listed below. For some questions you need a 'yes' answer, for other questions you need a 'no' answer. Write down the name of the pupil.

Example:

Find someone who …

… likes strawberry ice-cream

Find someone who …	needed answer	name:
1. … likes broccoli	....	....
2. … loves spinach	....	....
3. … doesn't eat meat	....	....
4. … is allergic to some kind of food	....	....
5. … eats raw carrots	....	....
6. … doesn't drink milk	....	....
7. … eats one hamburger every week	....	....
8. … drinks one litre of water every day	....	....
9. … eats one piece of fruit every day	....	....
10. … doesn't spend money on sweets	....	....

Now write a report about what you found out about your classmates. You can start like this:

I found out that ………………………………………… (name) likes broccoli. …

EXTRA

A. Make an alphabet of fruits and vegetables. Example: **A:** apple, **B:** banana, **C:** cauliflower, **D:** dried fruit, **E:** …

B. What are your favourite fruits and vegetables? Make a "TOP 5" list for each one.

C. How healthy do you eat? Look at the points 1–10 above and write about yourself.

7.1 Making plans for the weekend

1. Things to do in Edinburgh

Read about Edinburgh's attractions. Where would you like to go for a day or for the weekend?

---

www.eica-ratho.com

EICA: Ratho

The Edinburgh International Climbing Arena: Ratho, is built around a natural rock face. It is the world's largest indoor climbing arena attracting climbers of all stages; from beginner to expert. It has three large climbing walls, over 250 routes.

---

www.dynamicearth.co.uk

Our Dynamic Earth

– it's the Mother Earth of all adventures! Explore our planet's past, present and future. You'll be shaken by volcanoes, fly over glaciers, feel the chill of polar ice, and even get caught in a tropical rainstorm. Discover Scotland's geological heritage in our brand new gallery. In the new FutureDome you can travel forward in time.
Opening times 10.00am – 6.00pm

---

www.stjamesshopping.com

St James Shopping Centre

St James Shopping is located in the city centre and offers shoppers a wide range of stores. Shoppers can relax and catch up with friends over a coffee at the Costa café, or have a bite to eat in 'Food on 1' or 'The Place to Eat' restaurants.

Opening hours:
Monday – Thursday   9am – 6pm
Friday   9am – 8pm
Saturday   9am – 6pm

EDINBURGH ZOO

Edinburgh Zoo opened in 1913. Today the Zoo is home to over 1,000 rare and beautiful animals from around the world.
There are so many fascinating animals to visit at the Zoo! You can visit the new chimpanzee enclosure, or touch the colours of the rainbow with the interactive, Rainbow Lorikeet (= kind of parrots) enclosure. Or you can watch the UK's only koalas or waddle with the penguins in the world famous Penguin Parade. There are also many play areas for children, restaurants and a gift shop.
Open every day of the year, even Christmas Day!
– Just ten minutes from the centre of Edinburgh.

---

rock face *Felswand* – **haven** *Hafen, hier: Paradies* – **store** *shop* – **wide range** *many vielfältiges Angebot* – **to catch up with sb** *sich auf den neuesten Stand bringen, sich austauschen* – **to explore** *erkunden* – **glacier** *Gletscher* – **chill** *Kälte* – **to discover** *entdecken* – **geological heritage** *geologisches Erbe (Gegebenheiten)* – **gallery** *exhibition (Ausstellung)* – **enclosure** *Gehege* – **to waddle** *watscheln* – **gift** *Geschenk (Souvenir)*

2. Something for everyone!

Read about Chris, Sarah, Pauline and David. Where do the children like to go?

name	Chris	Sarah	Pauline	David
place				

Chris is 12 years old and he likes science. When his dad has enough time, they often go to museums and exhibitions. Chris wants to find out everything. He often makes experiments with his children's home lab. His favourite subjects are maths, geography and biology.

Sarah is 13 years old and she's a real sports fan. Most of all she likes PE. In her free time she plays in a girls' hockey team and she often goes jogging with her dad and sometimes they spend a weekend skiing in the mountains. Last year she also discovered climbing and loved it at once.

Pauline is 12 years old and she's an animal lover. At home she has got a dog, two cats and a rabbit. She lives on a farm. In her free time she likes going to the zoo because there she can watch a lot of animals from other continents. Her favourites are penguins. She would like to have one for herself.

David is 12 years old and he is very stylish. Clothes are very important to him. So he spends a lot of his pocket money on new outfits. He likes strolling through markets and second-hand shops because it's cheaper. But sometimes he also likes going to a shopping centre.

3. Let's talk: What are you doing this weekend?

a) Sarah and her friend Neil want to spend a day together. Read the dialogue.

Sarah: Have you made any plans for the weekend yet?

Neil: No, I haven't. But what about a visit to the shopping centre?

Sarah: Oh no! That's boring. And I don't want to spend my pocket money on useless stuff. Have you ever been climbing? I'd rather do that.

Neil: No, I haven't. Have you?

Sarah: Yes, of course. I go there once a week and it's really good. Let's go to Ratho on Saturday. Neil: Sounds good, but can I climb and what do I need?

Sarah: Don't worry. I'll show you the easy climbs and I'm sure you'll have fun. You don't need anything special. I can give you a pair of my climbing shoes.

Neil: Great. When do we go?

Sarah: What about Saturday at about 10 a.m.? Let's meet at the bus stop in front of your house. We'll be back at about 4 p.m. Is that OK?

Neil: Perfect. See you Saturday.

b) Work with a partner and make up a dialogue.

to discover *entdecken* – **at once** *sofort* – **to stroll** *bummeln*

Let's talk: Meeting a friend

1. Alex meets Emma

Read the dialogue and choose the best answer. Tick (✓). Look at Alex' questions for help.

Alex: Hi Emma! What are you doing?
Emma: ☐ a) I'm going to the library.
☐ b) I'm walking to the book shop.
☐ c) I'm having an ice-cream with friends.

Alex: Why are you going to the book shop?
Emma: ☐ a) I have to buy a birthday present.
☐ b) I'm looking for new books.
☐ c) I want a book about Golden Retrievers.

Alex: Are they your favourite animals?
Emma: ☐ a) Yes, they definitely are.
☐ b) No, I can't say that.
☐ c) Cats and dogs are my favourite animals.

Alex: Have you got one?
Emma: ☐ a) No, but maybe I'll get one next year.
☐ b) b) No, I haven't.
☐ c) c) Yes, I got one for my birthday.

Alex: May I come and see it?
Emma: ☐ a) Yes, that's a good idea.
☐ b) I don't think that's a good idea.
☐ c) I have to ask my parents first.

Alex: When can I come to your place?
Emma: ☐ a) You can come tonight.
☐ b) You can come now.
☐ c) You can come tomorrow morning.

Alex: OK, then. See you tomorrow.
Emma: ☐ a) That's all right.
☐ a) It's OK.
☐ a) Bye.

EXTRA

Use the phrases above and make up a dialogue with a partner. Choose one of these situations:

A. You meet a friend in front of a pet shop. He/she would like to have a rabbit pet but his/her parents say no.

B. You meet a classmate who is taking three dogs for a walk. Find out whose dogs they are and why he/she is looking after them.

C. You meet a boy/girl you really like. You would like to spend some time with him/her.

Let's talk: Meeting friends

Role cards: Meeting friends

Find a partner. Choose a situation. Make little dialogues and act them out.

At a supermarket A
• Begrüßung
• Erkundige dich, warum er/sie hier einkauft.
• Frage, was er/sie einkaufen möchte.
• Sage, dass du auch fürs Abendessen einkaufen musst, Brot, Butter, Käse und Salat. Frage, ob dein Partner auch eine Einladung zu Sashas Geburtstag hat.
• Schlage einen Kinobesuch vor.
• Schlage den Kauf einer Musik CD vor.
• Erwidere die Verabschiedung.

At a supermarket B
• Begrüßung
• Sage, dass du mit deinem Vater hier bist.
• Sage, dass ihr fürs Abendessen Gemüse braucht und du auch nach einem Spiel Ausschau hältst. Frage nach der Einkaufsliste des Partners.
• Bejahe dies und schlage vor, gemeinsam nach einem Geschenk zu suchen.
• Sage, dass Sasha nicht gern ins Kino geht.
• Sage, dass das eine gute Idee ist. Verabschiede dich.

In front of the cinema A
• Begrüßung
• Frage, was dein Freund hier macht.
• Sage, dass du Animationsfilme gut findest.
• Stimme zu. Verabredet euch.
• Verabschiedung

In front of the cinema B
• Begrüßung
• Sage, dass du für Freitag einen Film suchst.
• Frage, ob dein Freund Lust hat mitzugehen.
• Sage, dass du deinen Freund abholen kannst.
• Verabschiedung

In front of the leisure centre A
• Begrüßung
• Sage, dass du dich freust, deinen Freund hier zu sehen.
• Sage, dass du auch ins Schwimmbad willst. Schlage vor, gemeinsam reinzugehen.
• Frage, ob er/sie oft hierher kommt.
• Sage, dass du auch gerne schwimmst und ihr euch für nächste Woche auch verabreden könnt.
• Bestätige den Termin und verabschiede dich.

In front of the leisure centre B
• Begrüßung
• Frage, was er/sie hier machen will. Sage, dass du schwimmen gehst.
• Sage, dass das eine gute Idee ist. So ist es nicht so langweilig.
• Sage, dass du jede Woche einmal ins Schwimmbad gehst.
• Verabrede dich für nächste Woche.
• Erwidere die Verabschiedung.

Three students – who is who?

There are three exchange students waiting at the train station. You pick them up, but first you have to find out who's who and what colour the dresses and the rucksacks are.

Read all the clues and fill in the girls' names and the colours in the table below.

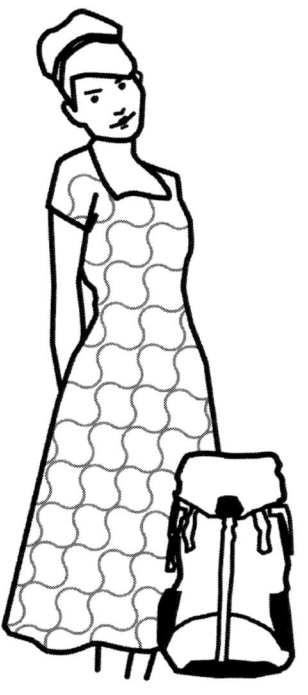  

1. Annabel isn't wearing the green dress.
2. The girl with the orange dress is standing on the right, next to the girl with the pink dress. Pauline has got a blue rucksack.
3. The yellow rucksack belongs to Emma.
4. Pauline is standing next to Annabel.
5. The green dress is not Emma's.
6. The girl with the orange dress is not standing next to the girl with the green dress.
7. Next to the girl with the orange dress is the girl with the black rucksack.

name			
colour of dress			
colour of rucksack			

Now you can colour the picture in the right colours.

Let's read: Strange neighbours

Strange neighbours – who is who?

You are walking along the street where every house has a different colour and all the people living there have got unusual pets. Suddenly you spot a crocodile that is lost. It can't find its home. You must help. Be a detective and find out, where the crocodile lives. Read all the clues first. Then solve the riddle and colour the houses.

1. The French person lives in the red house.
2. The Italian man has got a wolf.
3. The Polish man likes to eat potatoes.
4. The white house is on the right, next to the green house. The owner of the green house likes to eat pears.
5. The man who likes climbing has got a bear. The house in the middle is red. The man who lives there likes to eat apples.
6. The owner of the yellow house plays volleyball.
7. The Scotsman lives in the first house.
8. The Scotsman's neighbour plays badminton. He lives next to the man with a rabbit. The man who owns a penguin lives next to the volleyball player.
9. The rugby player likes to eat cucumbers.
10. The Scotsman lives next to the blue house.
11. The German likes mountain biking.
12. The badminton player has got a neighbour who likes to eat tomatoes.

House no.	1	2	3	4	5
Colour					
Nationality					
Food					
Animal					
Sport					

Opposites – adjectives

12

1. What's the opposite of ...?

Which two adjectives are opposites? Find the pairs and draw lines.

exciting	light	cheap	tiny	safe	nervous	beautiful	lazy
dark	huge	boring	expensive	ugly	dangerous	busy	calm

difficult	sunny	slow	early	clean	long	heavy	bad
easy	fast	dirty	cloudy	late	short	good	light

2. Which opposite pair fits?

Use some of the opposite pairs from exercise 1 to fill in the gaps.

1. When you write a test you are _nervous_ but you should better be _calm_.
2. Elephants are _____ animals, whereas mice are _____ .
3. When I get up at 7o'clock it's _____ outside, when I go to bed it's _____ .
4. It was bright and _____ in the morning but now it is getting _____ .
5. I have to get up _____ in the morning, only on Sundays I can sleep _____ .
6. Your schoolbag is _____ compared to your pencil case which is _____ .
7. In winter the days are are _____ and the nights are _____ .
8. When you fall into mud, you get _____ . After you wash and change clothes you are _____ again.
9. It's _____ to walk over a frozen lake. It's not _____ at all.
10. If you travel by ICE, you'll be very _____ . If you use regional trains, you'll be rather _____ .

3. A partner quiz

a) Write down five adjectives. Let your partner find a suitable opposite.
b) Write a sentence and use two opposite adjectives.

whereas wohingegen, während – **mud** Matsch – **frozen** gefroren – **rather** ziemlich – **suitable** passend

Opposites – Pictionary

Teacher's copy

How to play Pictionary with opposites:

Cut out cards and put them into a file, upside down. Divide class into two teams. Each team may choose a team name which you write on the board to keep track of points.

A member of team A comes to the front and picks a card. He/she then has to draw pictures that illustrate the given word pair within 60 seconds.

The other members of team A have to figure out the right answer to score a point.

When the time ends before the team has guessed the word pair, it's team B's turn.

Give an example, e.g. draw pictures for huge (e.g. elephant) – tiny (e.g. mouse) on the board and ask pupils to guess the adjectives.

long – short	beautiful – ugly
tall – small	empty – full
happy – sad	south – north
young – old	left – right
fat – thin	XL (extra large) – XS (extra small)
sweet – sour	light – heavy
hot – cold	wet – dry
slow – fast	good – bad
sunny – cloudy	strong – weak
easy – difficult	poor – rich
east – west	sour – sweet
quiet – loud	huge – tiny

14

A crossword (relative clauses)

1. A crossword

Read the clues and fill in the words.

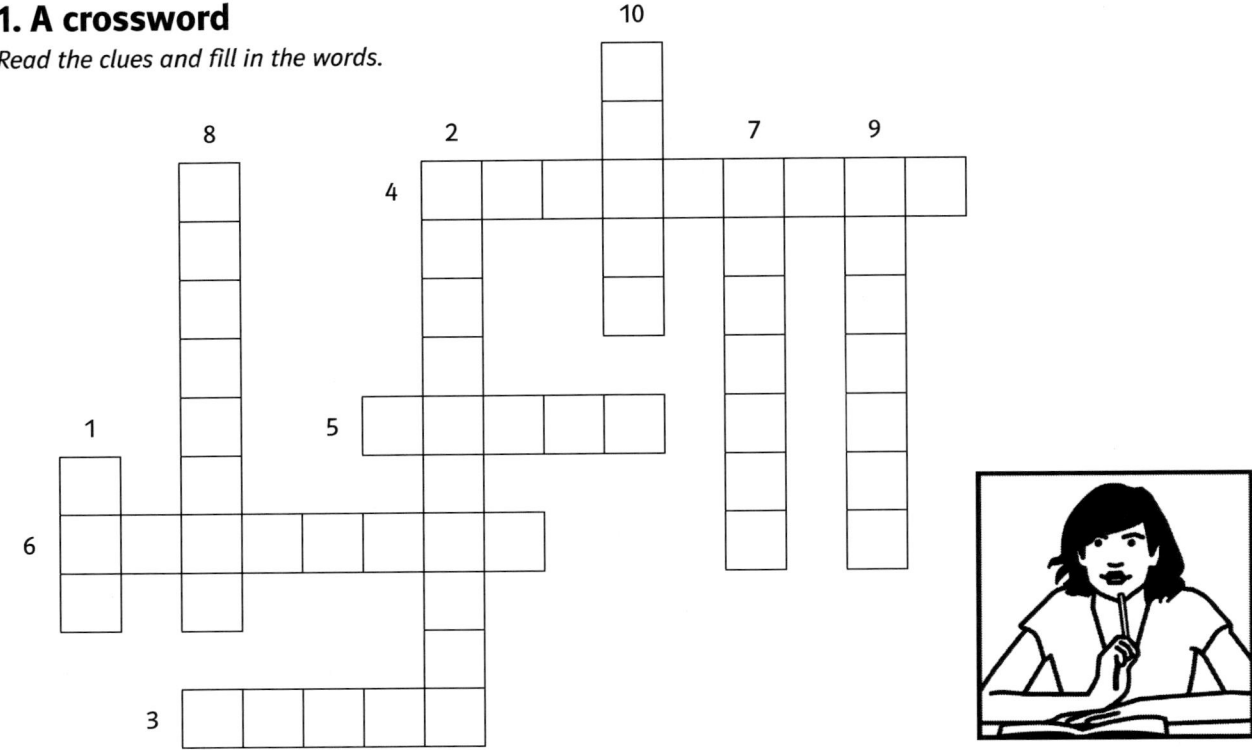

1. A thing which you have in your pencil case and you write with it.
2. A book which tells you the meaning of words.
3. A person who is not your friend.
4. A police officer who finds out information about a crime and arrests criminals.
5. A meal which comes from Italy. It is baked in the oven and has salami, tuna or vegetables and cheese on it.
6. An animal which is large, heavy and grey and lives in Africa and India.
7. An instrument which is made of metal and you must blow into it.
8. An electronic device which you need for writing texts and e-mails and for playing games.
9. People who lived in the North of Europe 1,000 years ago. They were famous for their ships and discovered America.
10. England has one. She wears a crown on her head.

2. A quiz for a partner

a) Think of three words and write a clue for them. Use relative clauses.

1. ....
2. ....
3. ....

b) Swap clues with your partner. Can you guess each other's words?

EXTRA

Make your own crossword. Swap crosswords with a partner.

Dictionary skills: All in alphabetical order

1. What animals do you like?

a) Write down your eight favourite animals. You can check the spelling in a dictionary.

....
....
....
....

b) Now put your favourite animals into alphabetical order.

....
....
....
....

2. A, B, C, …

Put the letters into alphabetical order.

G – L – O – E – Y – J – A – F – B – M – S – U

....

3. Look closely!

The words all start with the same letter. Number them in the right alphabetical order.

☐ invent – ☐ interest – ☐ island – ☐ international – ☐ invite – ☐ interview – ☐ interesting

4. What's the alphabetical order?

Put the words on the left in the right position. Draw arrows.

beaver	**beach**
beautiful	**beat**
bee	**become**
behaviour	**bedroom**
beauty	**begin**
belly button	**behind**
bell	**belly**

5. How do these words sound?

Can you read these words? Say them out loud and write them down.

[skuːl]   [friːz]   [kliːn]   [lʌnʃ]   [ˈskeəri]

....

16.1

1. Do you know these verbs?

Write down the English word for the German verbs. You can use a dictionary for help.

1. gehen – ....
2. fühlen – ....
3. machen (2) – ....
4. sich unterhalten (2) – ....
5. schwimmen – ....
6. sprechen – ....
7. nehmen – ....
8. zuhören – ....
9. schreiben – ....
10. geben – ....
11. spielen – ....
12. bezahlen – ....
13. überraschen – ....
14. flüstern – ....

2. Hidden verbs

Find the English verbs from exercise 1 in the word search. ↓↑ ⇆ ↗

A	E	M	X	V	F	O	J	M	P	G	K	T	P	L
X	K	A	J	F	I	P	L	K	X	I	A	E	L	O
C	E	K	I	C	X	V	H	T	Q	V	K	P	A	Y
V	R	E	K	W	G	U	E	L	E	E	F	N	Y	D
M	W	O	W	H	I	S	P	E	R	J	A	H	I	G
N	Q	D	R	G	O	I	D	G	L	U	P	F	D	A
Z	E	T	O	J	L	K	A	S	E	M	N	E	V	E
U	T	G	A	S	W	D	U	K	B	V	E	R	S	C
O	I	B	C	X	R	J	A	Y	G	A	V	I	O	R
S	R	A	N	Q	G	T	H	Z	V	Z	R	H	A	M
S	W	I	M	D	S	Y	B	M	E	P	Y	A	Z	P
P	S	E	R	A	M	A	S	Y	R	U	A	T	K	I
E	W	I	P	T	K	D	E	U	D	A	E	L	S	S
A	R	H	A	Z	L	I	S	T	E	N	L	R	I	D
K	F	H	Y	E	A	A	G	W	H	Q	E	P	O	E
S	C	K	M	F	T	G	Z	A	J	S	U	P	U	D

Verbs, verbs, verbs

3. Which verb?

Choose the right verb from exercise 1 to go with these phrases.

1. .... the homework
2. .... to strangers in a chat room
3. .... in the lake every afternoon
4. .... swimming
5. .... the cold breeze in the face
6. .... the patient some medicine
7. .... volleyball once a week
8. .... slowly, so that I can understand you
9. .... a story about a castle
10. .... at the cash desk
11. .... a secret to your friend
12. .... your mum on her birthday
13. .... to your favourite songs
14. .... the bus
15. .... a cake

EXTRA

Make a word search for a partner. Hide the English words for these German ones:

kaufen – verkaufen – lesen – sammeln – rennen – sich treffen – essen – schlafen – trinken – singen

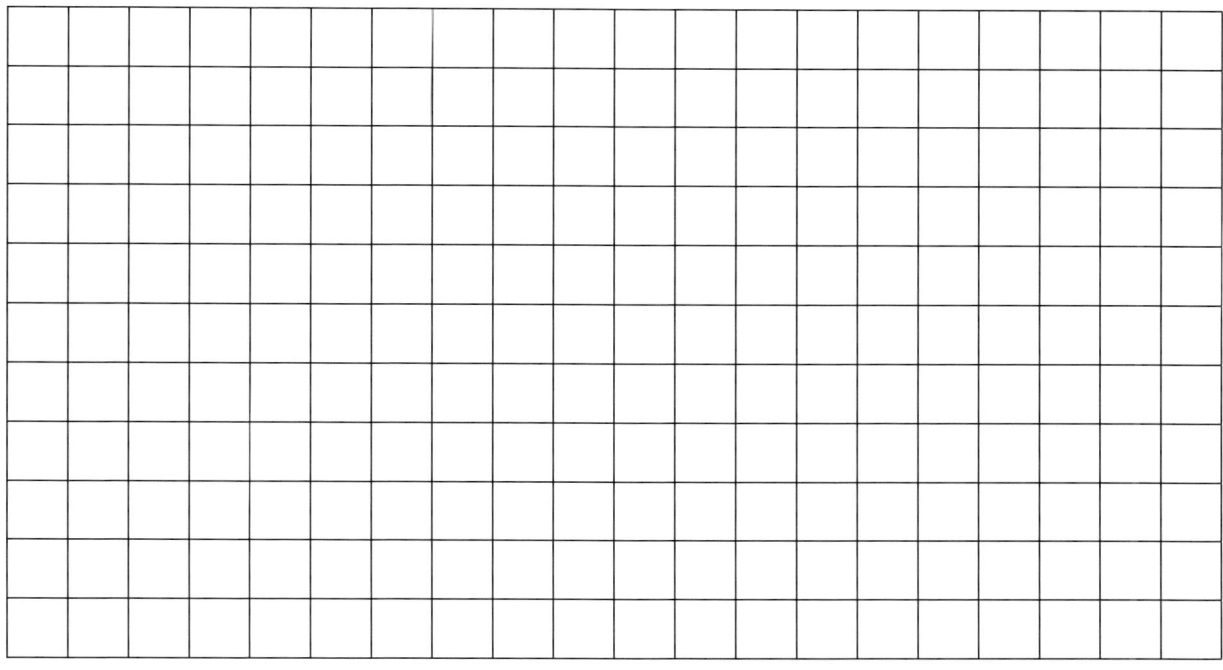

17 Irregular verbs – a maze

1. A maze

You have to find the three verb forms of the irregular verbs to get through this maze. When you come to a word that is not an irregular verb, you have to find another way. ⇅ ⇆

START ↓

go ↓ went	alone → gone	jump sky	angel volleyball
woke woken	wake ↓ feel	radio felt	smile felt
son ate	music eat	took taken	take rap
eaten think	found find	found made	make made
thought tea	thought see-saw	see saw	sea seen

↓ **FINISH**

2. Sort the verbs!

Copy all the irregular verbs from exercise 1 into a table like this:

infinitve	simple past	past participle	German
go	went	gone	

EXTRA

Work with a partner. Sit face to face. Take turns playing the game:

Partner A: Clap your hands, then your arms, then your legs. Repeat this until you have found a rhythm.

Partner B: Before A claps his hand, say one of the verbs below. Your partner has to say the simple past form and the past participle form while clapping.

think – feel – make – take – be – eat – find – let – wake – get – come – go – see

Irregular verbs – Once upon a time ...

1. Time for a fairy-tale

Do you know the story? Fill in the missing simple past forms of the verbs.

Once upon a time there **w** .... a queen who **t** .... Snow White **w** .... the most beautiful princess. She **w** .... to her house with a poisoned apple. When Snow White **a** .... the apple, she **f** .... asleep. The seven dwarves **w** .... very sad when they **f** .... her because they **t** .... she **w** .... dead. They **m** .... a glass coffin and when a prince **c** .... by and **s** .... her he **f** .... in love with her. When the dwarves **t** .... the coffin to the castle they almost **l** .... it fall and then Snow White **w** .... up again, spitting out the piece of poisoned apple. Soon after that, the prince and Snow White **g** .... married.

poisoned vergiftet – **drawf** Zwerg – **coffin** Sarg – **to spit out sth** etw. ausspucken

2. Train your memory!

Cut off the upper part of the worksheet. Read one sentence of the fairy-tale and turn the story face down. Now write down the sentence from your memory. Keep doing this until you have copied the whole story.

Now, can you tell the fairy-tale in your own words – without looking at the text?

1. Different feelings and moods

What moods are these people in? How are they feeling? Match the adjectives with the people.

friendly – silly – indifferent – shy – annoyed – bored – absent-minded – encouraging –

angry – frightened – thoughtful – amazed – relaxed – cheeky – tired – in love – sad – content

....

....

....

2. When do you feel angry, annoyed, tired, …?

Write at least three sentences. Examples: I'm friendly when I talk to a small child.
I feel tired when I go to bed late.

....

....

....

3. Let's mime and guess!

Work in groups of 4–5 pupils. One of you says one sentence in a certain mood. The others have to guess what mood it is. Take turns.

1. The film turned out to be boring.
2. Red is a wonderful colour.
3. I like my coffee hot with lots of milk.
4. I never go out when it's raining.
5. The shirt suits you.
6. I believe in miracles.
7. I've never been to London.
8. Go away with that cat.
9. Take the stairs instead of the lift.
10. Jogging is great.

Your 'Mood-o-Meter'

Make your own 'Mood-o-Meter' for the door of your room.

a) *Choose some of the phrases below and make up your own descriptions.*

- I feel fantastic!
- Please come in!
- Stay away. I'm in a bad mood.
- Disturb in an emergency only. I'm ...
- Keep quiet. I'm ...
- ...

Your ideas:

....
....
....
....

b) *Write the sentences of your choice on the first circle. Add "faces" to illustrate the different moods. Then cut out the two circles and use a paper fastener to put them together.*

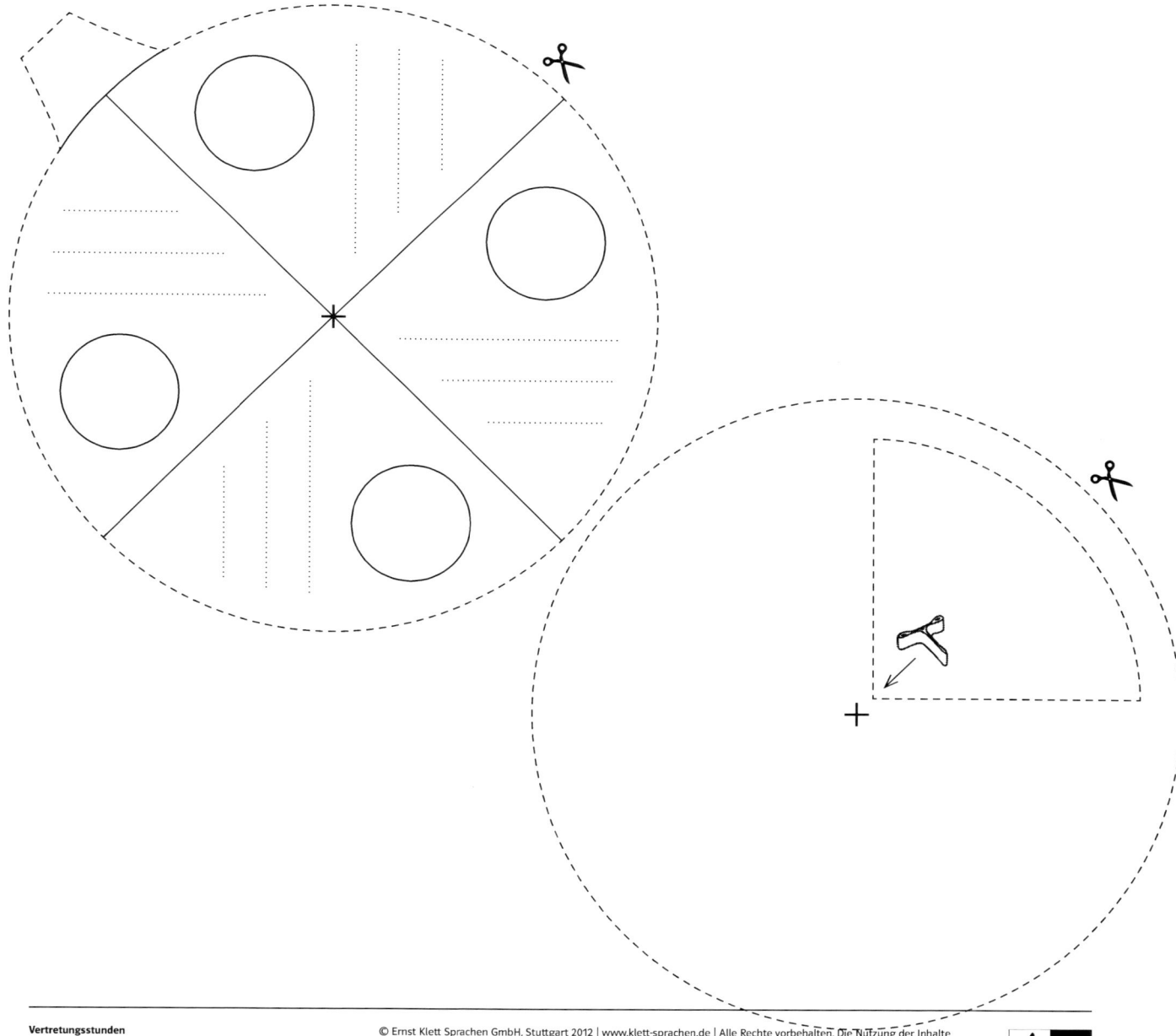

1. How do you like these foods?

Sort them into the table.

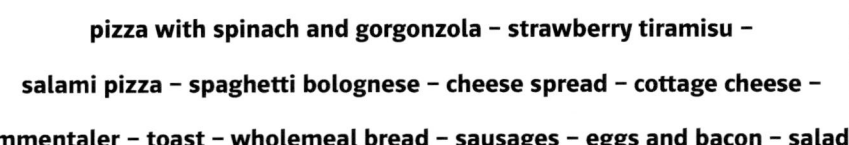

pizza with spinach and gorgonzola – strawberry tiramisu – salami pizza – spaghetti bolognese – cheese spread – cottage cheese – Emmentaler – toast – wholemeal bread – sausages – eggs and bacon – salad – potatoes – chips – fish – burger – apple – fruit salad – cake – biscuits – chocolate – cauliflower – aubergine – broccoli – smoothies – milkshake – ice-cream – yoghurt – buttermilk – steak – cornflakes – muesli – crisps – ...

delicious	packed with calories	don't like	healthy

2. Your eating habits

a) What do you eat in a normal day?

Breakfast: ....

Lunch: ....

Dinner: ....

Snacks: ....

b) Now look at your notes from a). How healthy do you think your meals are? What could you change to make them healthier? Add your ideas in a different colour.

c) Work with a partner. Listen to his/her diet. Give some useful advice. Take turns.

....
....
....
....
....
....

1. The 'Feed Me Better' campaign

Jamie Oliver – a well-known chef – started the 'Feed Me Better Campaign' in 2005. Here's what he says.

a) Read the text from his website. You may use a dictionary if necessary.

When I signed up as a dinner lady to make school dinners at Kidbrooke school in Greenwich, I wanted to show people what rubbish their kids were getting fed at school and how little government was spending. Basically, I wanted to get rid of the junk. I had to prove that, for the same price as a bag of crisps, just 37p, I could produce a properly cooked, nutritious meal at lunchtime. [...]

At Kidbrooke, the kids were eating a quarter of a ton of chips every week. The food budget was 37p per meal and Nora and her team of dinner ladies had become totally unmotivated by the food they served.

I needed a set of menus that we could serve to the 15,000 school children across Greenwich, for the same price, to set an example for the whole country and show the government it could be done. [...] To get the kids to accept the new food, all of the junk food including sweets and fizzy drinks had to be banned so there was no alternative.

It was one of the hardest things I've ever done but it worked. A year later, Nora's still serving the same food, the kids love it and they have a portion of fruit, and vegetables or salad with every meal.

So many kids still don't get a hot meal at lunch time and I wanted to help parents realize how much junk their kids are actually eating. Because if chocolate bars, fizzy drinks and crisps are part of their daily diet, they are going to face health problems later in life.

The Feed Me Better campaign was fantastic. I needed help to go to the government and get them to change, so I was asking for five things:

1. Guarantee that children receive a proper, nutritionally balanced meal on their plates.

2. Introduce nutritional standards and ban junk food from school meals.

3. Invest in dinner ladies: give them better kitchens, more hours and loads of support and training to get them cooking again.

4. Teach kids about food and get cookery back on the curriculum. (Kids need to be learning about food right from day one, so they aren't afraid of what food looks, smells and tastes like and where it comes from. Make cooking compulsory for ALL kids so they can survive and live on a budget when they leave school.)

5. Commit long-term funding to improve school food.

1 to sign up sich verpflichten – 4 to get rid of the junk den Plunder (das schlechte Essen) loswerden – 5 nutritious nahrhaft – 12 fizzy drink Brausegetränk – 18 diet Ernährung – 21 to guarantee garantieren – 21 nutritionally balanced ausgewogen – 25 curriculum Lehrplan – 27 compulsory verpflichtend – 28 to live on a budget sparsam sein müssen, nicht viel Geld zur Verfügung haben – 29 to commit long-term funding Langzeitfinanzierung bereitstellen

b) Decide whether the statements are true or false. Tick (✓) true or false.

	true	false
1. Jamie Oliver started his campaign in Greenwich.	☐	☐
2. His aim was to ban junk food.	☐	☐
3. In 2005, kids in GB ate a quarter of a ton of chips every day.	☐	☐
4. One meal can cost 37p.	☐	☐
5. Sweets and fizzy drinks are still available at schools.	☐	☐
6. The kids don't like the new meals.	☐	☐
7. With a healthy lunch kids will probably have fewer health problems in later life.	☐	☐
8. Cooking classes should take place in every school.	☐	☐

2. What does "junk food" mean?

Explain in your own words.

....

....

....

3. Your opinion – choose a task:

1. Imagine you come to school one morning and there's someone checking your lunch box. If he or she finds junk food or fizzy drinks, it will be thrown away immediately. What do you think?

2. Describe the lunch you like best. What (kind of food) would you like to have in your lunch box? Give reasons for your choices.

EXTRA

A. Find out more about Jamie Oliver on the Internet. Make a fact file or write a short biography.

B. Work in groups and create a healthy school menu for Monday–Friday.

C. Is there a cafeteria at your school? Write about it. Here are some questions to help you:

- What's on the menu?
- How do you like the food?
- What do you like best?

A map of Scotland

Read about the different places and find them on the map. Fill in the right numbers.

10 Edinburgh

Edinburgh is Scotland's capital, has over 470,000 inhabitants and is a cosmopolitan and dynamic city. It's famous for its impressive castle and historic Old Town. In August the largest arts festival in the world takes place there.

1 Ben Nevis

With its 4,406 ft Ben Nevis is Scotland's and Britain's highest peak. A path leads up to Glen Nevis, but you must be a good hiker to reach the top. Other activities around the Nevis Range are paragliding, mountain biking and skiing in winter.

9 Glasgow

With over 600,000 people, Glasgow is the largest city and has a lively cultural and social life. It used to be a grey industrial place but has turned into a colourful urban centre. The city is located on the River Clyde, in southwest Scotland.

2 Aberdeen

Up north, Aberdeen is a city made of silvery granite. Its wealth comes from the North Sea oil.

3 The Scottish Borders

Sandwiched between England in the south and Edinburgh in the north, you'll find rolling hills, ruined abbeys and farmland – that's the Borders.

8 Loch Ness

Very deep, 23 miles long, cold and moody – that's Loch Ness, a lake surrounded by rugged mountains and inhabited by Nessie, the well-known monster.

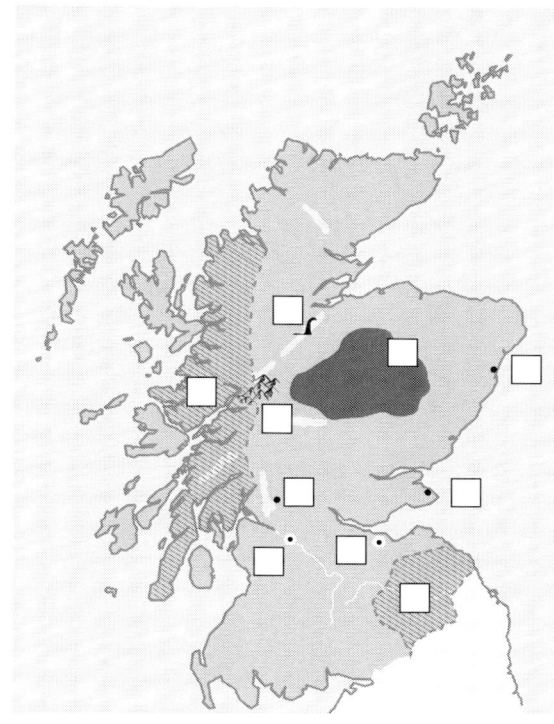

4 The Cairngorms National Park

The Cairngorm massif shows the raw wilderness of the Scottish Highlands.

7 Stirling

Stirling lies in the heart of Scotland and has a great castle from which you can see snowcapped Highland peaks as well as Edinburgh.

6 Argyll – Wester Ross

On the west coast from Argyll in the south to Wester Ross in the north you find the typical jagged coastline with the rugged Highlands in the back.

5 St Andrews

St Andrews lies on the east coast and is a famous university town. It's also home to Scotland's favourite game: golf.

EXTRA

A. *Write true/false statements for a partner.*

B. *Write down six quiz questions for a partner.*

A) Shinty – a Challenging Outdoor Sport

Shinty is a very old Scottish game that is played all over Scotland, but is especially popular in the Highlands. It is played with a stick and a ball, similar to hockey. In the game two teams of twelve players, including a goalkeeper, try to score goals. There is a lot of movement on the playing field which is 140 to 170 yards long. The players swing a stick, which is called caman. The wooden stick is about 3 1/2 ft long and has a curved end. The ball is about the size of a tennis ball. The players can use both ends of the stick to hit the ball and to block and to tackle the opponent. They are not allowed to touch the ball with their hands. Only the goalkeeper may use his hands but he may not catch the ball. Playing the ball with the head constitutes a foul. A game lasts 90 minutes and consists of two halves of 45 minutes – and the game is fast and furious.

B) The Edinburgh Festival

Every year in August, Edinburgh changes to a buzzing city during the festival. From the city's great concert halls to pubs and streets – everywhere you'll find a packed programme of entertainment. You can watch dramas or comedies in the theatres, listen to rock, pop, jazz, blues or traditional Scottish music in the streets and in the pubs. The streets are full of buskers, circus acts and craft stalls. The festival is visited by local people, tourists from all over the world, artists, musicians, and journalists. Pubs and restaurants have extended opening hours and the atmosphere in town is lively. The Edinburgh Festival began in 1947. Rudolf Bing had the idea of playing music from various central European countries. At the same time eight theatre groups performed in the city without being invited. This was the birth of the Edinburgh Festival, an annual series of various festival events.

C) Historic Ales

Scotland is famous for malt whisky – but also for beer. Traditional Scottish beer is a thick, dark ale, served at room temperature in pints or half-pints. There are some local breweries that still brew historic ales with gooseberry, seaweed, pine, elderberry or heather. Heather Ale – called Fraoch – is a refreshing drink sold in bottles. It's a light yellow and brown-coloured ale with a spicy herbal flavour. Highlanders started brewing that beer around 2,000 B.C. and nowadays it is the oldest ale still produced in the world. The old Celtic druids studied the art of brewing ales very well. When the malted barley is boiling, sweet berries and flowering heather are added. As soon as the cooling process begins, the hot ale is poured into a vat of fresh heather flowers where it remains for an hour, before the fermentation process starts.

D) Dolphins of the Moray Firth

The Moray Firth, the large bay northeast of Inverness where the Highlands meet the North Sea, is an area where bottle-nosed dolphins can be spotted easily from the shore or a boat. It is the most northernly breeding ground for the bottle-nosed dolphin in Europe.
The best time to watch some of the estimated 150 wonderful mammals is probably the hour before high tide, when fish are close to the surface and the hungry animals follow them. The dolphins usually live in herds of ten to thirty members and they can grow up to four metres in length. However, researchers warn that the number of animals is constantly declining: too much boat traffic makes the dolphins nervous and overalert. Especially in the breeding time the stress level is too high for the dolphins and their calves. They have to remain underwater for too long periods. Other dangers are pollution and as a result less food.

Blackfeet Metal Warriors

The Blackfeet reservation lies in Montana, on the foothills of the Rocky Mountains, the holy and sacred mountains for the Blackfeet. Its size is about the size of Germany and Browning is its centre. Browning lies in the Great Plains where buffalo were hunted in former times. The troublesome history of the Blackfeet nation forced them to settle down – but such a life is a big contrast to the traditional, nomad way of living. Today Blackfeet lead a modern life with supermarkets, Internet, cars and they live in mobile homes or wooden houses. Blackfeet have a different way of organizing their household and garden as well as getting rid of old things. So (German) visitors often find two or three old, rusted cars standing around in the garden. Blackfeet artist Jay Laber took scraps of such rusted cars, pick up trucks and busses as well as stones of an old mission school to create the metal warriors. When Jay works on his creations, he does the same thing his forefathers had done centuries ago: He makes use of things and materials that are available in the natural environment: the cars and other trash objects he finds in his surroundings, left behind by people. He is a skilled artist who turns metal junk into life by twisting, carving, cutting and welding it. The two native warriors sit on their horses that are made of the materials mentioned above. They look proud and stand at the four entrances to the Blackfeet reservation to welcome visitors. If you take a closer look at the sculptures, you can discover everything a warrior represents: responsibility to family and friends, but also to nature and the creator, humility, the power of giving and spirituality. There are different ways of living on our planet, have a look at the Blackfeet way – that's what they want to express.

Miss Blackfeet

"Oki", hello, my name is Rose Mad Stone. I'm the Miss Blackfeet for the Blackfeet Nation for this year. My Indian name is "Ancient Song". I'm a junior at the Browning High School. My goals are to complete High School and to go on to college to study law.
My parents are Bill and Betty Mad Stone. I have two brothers (Jared and Jason) and one sister Tracy. My paternal grandparents are the late Emery Mad Stone and Elizabeth Guardipee Mad Stone. My great-grandparents are Melvin and Agatha (Chewing Blackbone) Mad Stone. My great-great grandfather was Chewing Blackbone. My maternal grandparents are the late Robert Weatherwax, Sr. and Margaret Stillsmoking. My greatgrandparents were Peter Weatherwax, Sr. and Mary Day Rider and Dave Stillsmoking, Sr. and Kathleen Spotted Bear Stillsmoking. I represent the Blackfeet Nation with great pride and honor. Today we live in an ever changing and challenging world. I too live in two worlds, my traditional background and the present. It is very important for young people to know their culture and past. They need to be proud of themselves and get a good education. My message to the people is to follow your dreams and make good choices.

Indian Relay Races: Extreme Warrior Contest

The rules of Indian Extreme Warrior Relay are simple. Teams consist of four people and three horses. In Browning, the rider first runs a certain distance, then there's a swimming contest, then he takes off his clothes and shoes and changes into traditional clothes and moccasins. The riding can start now. A team's rider makes three laps around the track, changing to a new horse at the beginning of each lap. Two teammates stand at the edge of the track holding and calming the waiting horses for the incoming rider. The fourth teammate's job is to catch the arriving horse while the rider dismounts and leaps onto the next horse. A perfect exchange is beauty in motion. The rider leaps off his horse and bounces one or two steps before vaulting on to the next horse and hugging its neck tightly as it takes off for another lap. But with 24 people and 18 horses all working in an area about the size of a basketball court, complications are common. Horses get excited and start dragging their holders around. Horses throw riders, rearing or taking off before the rider has a firm hold. Bumps and bruises are common, and broken bones are not unusual.

Young Blackfeet view the event as a cultural and spiritual connection to their forefathers, to warfare and hunting. It also makes them proud of themselves. To be a relay jockey means to lead a clean and healthy life. The traditional moccasin is so valuable to the rider in the photo that he doesn't want to loose it. So he keeps it in his mouth until the race is over.

North American Indian Days

The celebration in Browning is always held in the second week of July and lasts four days. It is an interesting way to see authentic Blackfeet traditions such as dancing (powwow), stick games, and horse relay races. Tipis and tents are put up on the powwow grounds for four days of contest dancing, games, a number of sports events and socializing. Once you hear and feel the rhythm of the drum, see the traditional and fancy dancing, and the many proud Native people, then you will begin to understand the Blackfeet Nation. Everyone is welcome and encouraged to attend the contest dancing. The dancers wear traditional clothes, not costumes. Costumes are for Halloween, the clothes worn by the dancers are hand

made, often passed down from generation to generation and crafted with some of the finest detail. Hundreds of hours or more go into the making of such a traditional outfit. There are drum and dance categories for all ages. Everyone who takes part in one of the contests has practised very hard throughout the year. The winners get prizes, e.g. the winner of the category "drums" gets 5,000$, the winner of the category "dance team boys and girls 12–18" gets 400$. Participating in such events is very important for young Blackfeet people.

Crazy sports

1. Crazy sports

Match the sports with their definitions. Fill in the right letters.

(A) speedminton   (B) frisbee golf   (C) zorbing
(D) underwater ice hockey   (E) extreme ironing
(F) sandboarding   (G) ice climbing   (H) snow biking
(I) bossaball

○ 1. Normally you do this at home. It's quite a dull activity done to reduce crinkles in your clothes.

○ 2. You do this sport in winter on frozen waterfalls. It's a kind of climbing.

○ 3. This fun sport can be practised anywhere outside. You need rackets and a ball. It's like badminton but you're not restricted by wind or rain. And it's fast.

○ 4. This fun sport is played in parks. It's similar to golf but you need a frisbee which you throw into baskets.

○ 5. To play this you need a puck made of styrofoam, a wetsuit, flippers and rackets, but no ice-skates. You play it in a pond (under the ice) in two teams.

○ 6. Skiing is nice, but to get a kick you use a kind of mountain bike with mini skis instead of wheels and down the hill you go.

○ 7. Snowboarding is great – and in summer? Try this kind of fun sport in the sand.

○ 8. Trampolining, beach volleyball, football and capoeira – all with South American bossa nova music! The court and the sides of the trampoline are padded so players won't get hurt. Sounds like a fun holiday activity at the beach, doesn't it?

○ 9. Rolling downhill in an orb – that is a big plastic ball – is called zorbing, globe-riding, sphereing or orbing. The rider is strapped inside the ball and then rolls down a slope.

EXTRA

A. a) What do you think of extreme or crazy sports? How far would you go? What's your favourite sport and why? Write a short text.

b) Work in groups of four. Discuss your texts.

B. Find some other crazy sports. Search the Internet or the school library. Write short definitions for at least two of them.

C. Invent a new crazy sport. Create a name for it and think up rules. Don't forget to give some safety tips.

A. At the bike rental

You are on an exchange visit in Great Britain with your class and some teachers.
The class wants to go on a bike trip. You were asked to find a bike rental and find out about prices and availability.
Act out the situation with a partner.

Assistant	You
• Begrüßung	
	• Begrüßung Du brauchst für eine Fahrradtour deiner Klasse (21 Schüler, zwei Lehrer) Fahrräder und möchtest diese gern leihen.
• Oh, das sind 23 Räder. Hm. Da musst du den Chef fragen. Bitte um einen Moment Geduld.	
	• Bei schönem Wetter wollt ihr übermorgen die Tour machen. Frage nach dem Preis.
• Gute Nachrichten: Ihr habt genug Fahrräder. Erkundige dich, wann die Tour geplant ist, weil ihr die Räder vor der Vermietung noch mal prüfen müsst.	
	• Ihr kommt vorbei. Frage, wann der Laden öffnet.
• Aha, übermorgen. Das ist gut. Sage, dass pro Rad und Tag £5 anfallen. Die Bezahlung erfolgt bei der Übergabe der Räder. Erkundige dich, ob die Fahrräder hier abgeholt werden oder an einen bestimmten Ort gebracht werden sollen.	
	• Bitte um eine Bestätigung der Ausleihe für deinen Lehrer.
• Geöffnet wird um 9.00 Uhr morgens, aber eine halbe Stunde früher ist auch o. k. Du bist sowieso hier. Kein Problem, hier ist sie.	
	• Bedanke dich. Verabschiede dich.
• Verabschiede dich.	

Let's talk: A bike trip

B. A bike trip

You are with your host parents. Ask for suggestions for a bike trip in the area. Act out the situation with a partner.

You	Host mum
• Sprich deine Gastmutter an und frage, ob du etwas fragen kannst.	• Bejahe und erkundige dich, worum es geht?
• Erkläre, dass du mit einigen anderen eine Radtour für übermorgen planen sollst. Du möchtest ein paar Tipps einholen.	• Sage, dass das eine super Idee ist. Das Wetter soll gut werden. Frage, ob sie zur Küste oder in die Gegenrichtung wollen.
• Vielleicht beides. Unterwegs soll es ein Picknick geben und wenn es geht, könnt ihr euch vielleicht auch noch irgendetwas anschauen.	• Hm. Du holst eine Karte und erklärst, dass sie deiner Wegbeschreibung folgen sollen. Frage, ob sie beim Radverleih in der Hauptstraße losfahren.
• Bestätige: Ja, das stimmt. Um 9.00 Uhr und ihr habt den ganzen Tag Zeit.	• Perfekt. Wenn ihr aus dem Zentrum raus seid, folgt ihr dem Coastal Bike Trail, der in ca. 1 Stunde zum Meer führt. Danach folgt ihr dem blauen Schild zum Leuchtturm. Da könnt ihr rasten und das kleine Museum besuchen.
• Erkundige dich, was das für ein Museum ist.	• Betone, dass das Museum wirklich interessant ist. Es zeigt die heimischen Pflanzen und Tiere, das ganze Ökosystem.
• Gut. Erkundige dich, wie es weiter geht.	• Beschreibe den Weg weiter: Ihr verlasst die Küste und folgt dem Radweg mit der roten Markierung. Der führt bergauf zu den Ruinen von Woodland Castle. Das ist ein perfekter Platz für ein Picknick und da gibt es einen großen Abenteuerspielplatz mit Boulderwänden und so.
• Erkläre, dass ihr zu alt für Spielplätze seid.	• Sei erstaunt und sage, dass du das nicht glaubst. Der Spielplatz wurde extra für eure Altersgruppe gebaut. Erkläre, dass Ron und Susan oder die anderen in der Schule das sicher bestätigen.
• O. k. Frage, wie es weiter geht.	• Folgt den roten Schildern und in einer weiteren Stunde werdet ihr zurück in der Stadt sein.
• Bedanke dich.	• Sage, dass du gern geholfen hast.

C. At the bike repair

Together with your class you have gone on a bike trip. You started with the others, but after the first kilometre the chain of your bike came off and you can't fix it yourself. Your teacher sends you back to the bike rental. Act out the situation with a partner.

Mechanic	You
• Begrüßung	• Begrüßung
• Erkundige dich, ob etwas am Fahrrad kaputt ist.	• Erkläre das Problem: Du verlierst ständig die Kette und dein Rad hat kein Reparaturset.
• Drücke Bedauern aus. Bitte den Kunden dort drüben zu warten während du das Rad reparierst.	• O. k., aber viel lieber möchtest du zusehen.
• Sage, dass das eine gute Idee ist, denn dann kannst du es das nächste Mal selber machen. Erkundige dich, woher der Schüler/die Schülerin kommt?	• Beantworte die Frage. (Nur der Name des Ortes reicht natürlich nicht.)
• Erfrage auch, bei wem er/sie wohnt.	• Antworte: Bei Familie Follan in der West Park Road.
• Erkundige dich, wie es ihm/ihr dort gefällt.	• Nett. Du wohnst da mit deinem/r Freund/in. Sage, dass es anstrengend ist, die ganze Zeit Englisch zu sprechen.
• Frage, wie lange die Klasse bleibt. Erkundige dich, ob er/sie vorhat, mal wieder zu kommen.	• Der Schüleraustausch dauert eine Woche, aber es sind leider nur noch zwei Tage übrig und dann kommt die lange Heimfahrt. Beantworte die Frage.
• Sage, dass du mit der Reparatur fertig bist.	• Frage, ob er dich zum Leuchtturm bringen kann. Deine Klasse wartet dort auf dich.
• O. k., das ist kein Problem. Aber den letzten Kilometer muss er/sie selber mit dem Rad fahren. Autos sind draußen im Nationalpark nicht erlaubt.	• Das ist schon in Ordnung. Bedanke dich.

In other words

1. Different words for the verb 'to go'

a) *Match the English verbs with their German translation. Draw lines.*
You can use a dictionary for help or to check your answers.

crawl	wandern
escape	eilen
hike	schlurfen
hurry	stapfen
limp	krabbeln
shuffle	gehen
stalk	bummeln
stroll	sich anpirschen, anschleichen
tramp	entkommen
walk	humpeln

b) *Find the most suitable word for each sentence.*

crawl – escape – hike – hurry – limp – shuffle – stalk – stroll – tramp – walk

1. If you don't have enough time, you must ....
2. If you have enough time, you can .... around the town.
3. If something frightens you, you'll try to ....
4. If it snowed throughout the night, you'd have to .... through the snow.
5. If you want to hunt an animal, you must .... it.
6. If there's something wrong with your leg, you'll ....
7. If the weather is fine, you can .... along the coast.
8. If you don't lift your feet properly, you ....
9. When you move on hands and feet, you ....
10. When you go for a long walk in the countryside, you ....

2. Odd one out

Which verb describes a different kind of movement? Circle the odd one out.

1. hurry – run – race – stroll
2. stalk – hurry – stroll – crawl
3. hike – limp – shuffle – trip over
4. shuffle – tramp – stalk – walk

1. The opposite of …

What are the opposites of these words? Sometimes there's more than one solution. If you need help, look at the box below.

1. active – ....
2. alive – ....
3. ancient – ....
4. awful – ....
5. best – ....
6. calm – ....
7. fabulous – ....
8. final – ....
9. careful – ....
10. loud – ....
11. optimistic – ....
12. poor – ....
13. private – ....
14. useful – ....

---
lazy – dead – modern – great, fantastic – worst – nervous, hyper – terrible, awful – first – careless – quiet – pessimistic – rich – public – useless

---

2. Which prefix?

The adjectives below form their opposites with the prefixes im-, il-, in- or un-.
Fill in the opposite with the help of a dictionary.

	im-	il-	in-	un-
possible				
polite				
friendly				
legal				
natural				
real				
spectacular				
successful				
active				
acceptable				

EXTRA

Use your dictionary again and write a list of seven adjectives. Swap lists with a partner and find suitable opposites.

Jeopardy game: All about adjectives

30.1

Play Jeopardy!

You play in two teams. One team starts by choosing a category and a number, e.g. **opposites 20**.
The quiz master reads the question hidden under **opposites 20**:

What is the opposite of private?

Now the team decides on one solution – a, b or c from the multiple choice answers read out by the quizmaster.

If the answer is correct, the team gets 20 points and can choose another question. If the answer is wrong, it's the other team's turn. The quizmaster counts the points each team achieves.

prefixes /suffixes	synonyms	opposites	extreme adjectives
10	10	10	10
20	20	20	20
30	30	30	30
40	40	40	40
50	50	50	50

Quizmaster's copy

	prefixes /suffixes	synonyms	opposites	extreme adjectives
10	What is the opposite of happy? a) inhappy b) imhappy c) **unhappy**	Find the synonym for delicious. a) sweet b) crunchy c) **yummy**	Find the opposite of active. a) **lazy** b) spectacular c) massive	What is the extreme form of happy? a) **cheerful** b) sad c) cheap
20	What is the opposite of careful? a) **careless** b) caring c) care-free	Find the synonym for ancient. a) **old** b) up to date c) new	Find the opposite of private. a) possible b) **public** c) popular	What is the extreme form of sad? a) horrible b) terrible c) **miserable**
30	What is the opposite of possible? a) unpossible b) ilpossible c) **impossible**	Find the synonym for expensive. a) cheap b) inexpensive c) **pricey**	Find the opposite of polite. a) **rude** b) unfamiliar c) cute	What is the extreme form of funny? a) very funny b) **hilarious** c) delicious
40	What is the opposite of honest? a) unhonest b) **dishonest** c) honestless	Find the synonym for chaotic. a) tasteless b) **disorganized** c) inorganized	Find the opposite of extraordinary. a) useful b) fantastic c) **normal**	What is the extreme form of tired? a) **exhausted** b) exhausting c) boring
50	What is the opposite of regular? a) unregular b) inregular c) **irregular**	Find the synonym for terrified. a) **scared** b) dangerous c) safe	Find the opposite of fabulous. a) **awful** b) scary c) successful	What is the extreme form of beautiful? a) good-looking b) **gorgeous** c) pretty

Dictionary skills: Look it up!

1. A, B, C, ...

Put the words into alphabetical order.

recollect – rectangular – recognize – reboot – reception – recent – receiver – recipient – recognizable – reassure – recycle – recommend – recreational

....

....

....

2. How to say it right

Look up the words and underline where the word is stressed. The little ['] will help you.

Example: recover   [rɪˈkʌvə] – re<u>co</u>ver

responsibility	handkerchief	successful
naturally	fortunately	impossible
international	endanger	energy
interesting	embarrassed	disposable

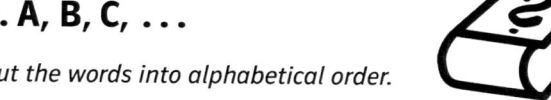

3. False friends

These words look and sound similar to German words – but they have a completely different meaning. Look up the German and English translations.

1. stool	–	2. Stuhl	–
3. strand	–	4. Strand	–
5. recipe	–	6. Rezept	–
7. (to) reclaim	–	8. reklamieren	–
9. tramp	–	10. Tramper	–
11. taste	–	12. Taste	–
14. brave	–	14. brav	–

4. What's the plural of ...?

Find the plural forms of the words below.

1. shelf	–	4. child	–
2. person	–	5. knife	–
3. wolf	–	6. mouse	–

1. Do you know the alphabet?

Put the words into alphabetical order. Number them.
(You can compete with a partner. Who can do the exercise the fastest?)

1. gratitude – greasy spoon – grave yard – greedy – grayish – green – gravity – gravel

2. slit – slip - slink – sliver – slight – sling – slim – slither

3. idle – icon – icing – ideogram – idealize – identical – idea – identify

4. path – paucity – patisserie – paternal – pathetic – patriot – pattern – patience

2. Headwords are important helpers

Headwords are the first and the last entries that are printed on a dictionary page. Headwords are different in every dictionary of course. They help you to find the word you are looking for quickly.

a) If the headwords are 'physiologist' and 'pictogram' which of these words can you find between them? Underline them.

physician – physiotherapist – physiognomy – pianissimo – picker – pictoral – picnic – picture

b) If the headwords are 'fragile' and 'free' which of these words can you find between them? Underline them.

fragment – fractional – fracture – fragrance – frailty – foxtrot – franchise – freak – freight

3. Geographical names

a) Look at the German words for the countries. Which ones are the same in English? Which ones change? Write them down and mark them with two different colours. Look them up in a dictionary to check.

b) Find the English words for the nationalities. Use your dictionary.

German	English country	English nationality
Sambia		
Namibia		
Kroatien		
Slowenien		
Nicaragua		
Norwegen		
Island		
Vietnam		

Dictionary skills: A bike

1. Bike words

a) *Do you know the English words? Look up all the words you don't know and label the picture.*

> Gangschaltung – Lenker – Vorderlicht – Bremse – Federung – Reflektor – Reifen – Rahmen – Pedal – Kette – Ventil – Rücklicht – Schutzblech – Sattel – Gepäckträger

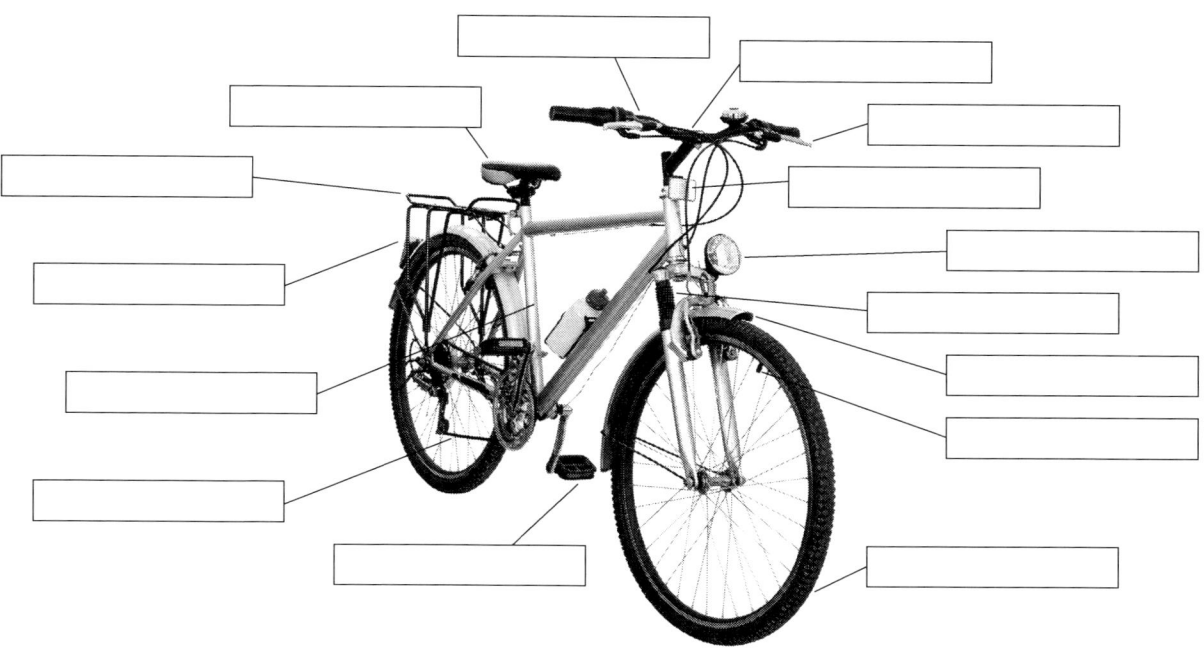

b) *What other bike words would you like to know? Look them up in a dictionary.*

2. What is it?

Read the definitions. What is it? Write down the right words.

1. The part of the bike you sit on: ....
2. The part of your bike that you hold with your hands: ....
3. You use it to carry things on your bike: ....
4. This object keeps the air in the tyre: ....
5. You need these when it's dark. They make you visible to others: ....
6. You need it to ride your bike the most effective way: ....

EXTRA: Creative writing

Choose one of the following tasks and write a text.

A. *What does your bike look like? Give a detailed description (in about 200 words).*

B. *What is your dream bike? Write about it and give a detailed description (in about 200 words).*

C. *Invent a new kind of bike. What is special about it? Write an advertisement.*

What do you know about Australia?

Work with a partner. Read the statements and decide if they are right (✓) or wrong (✗).

1. In 1926, the government of New South Wales was the first government in the world that paid pensions to women.

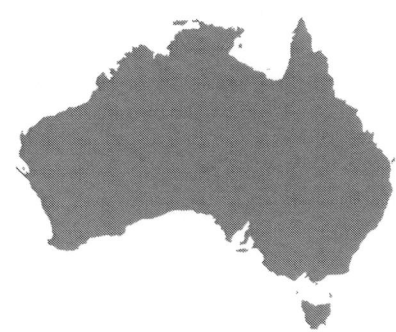

2. The first official world surfing championships were held in Sydney in 1964.

3. The Australian aeronautical research scientist David Warren invented the black box flight recorder for aircrafts in 1958.

4. Australian road train drivers who transport goods through the vast desert areas have to record the number of animals they kill on their way.

5. Eucalyptus was first used as a medicine by Aborigines, to treat coughs, fevers and asthma.

6. The longest fence in the world is located in Australia. It is 5,530 km long and was erected to keep dingoes away from sheep.

7. When Aborigines want to be near their ancestors, they spend the night on ghost trees.

8. The Royal Flying Doctor Service has more than 1,000 members of staff.

9. Melbourne's original name was Batmania after one of its founders John Batman.

10. Australia is the only continent without an active volcano.

11. Bungee jumping is originally an Australian kind of extreme sport.

12. When the first platypus was sent to England, the sceptical people believed the Australians had played a joke by sticking a duck's bill on a large rat's body.

13. Australia is the lowest continent in the world, with an average height of just 330 m above sea level.

14. Australia's first police force was created from a group of twelve of their best behaved convicts.

---

vast *huge, enormous* – **cough** *Husten* – **fence** *upright structure made of wire or wood that is put up around an area of land* – **to erect sth** *to construct or built sth* – **ancestor** *a family or tribe member who lived a long time ago* – **staff** *the people who work for a company or organization* – **founder** *someone who starts sth, e.g. a community or company* – **bill** *bird's beak (Schnabel)* – **convict** *prisoner*

The Simpson Desert Bike Challenge or Five Days in Hell

The Simpson Desert is located in the centre of Australia and it is a really unique desert wilderness. Mountain bike riders from all over the world go there every year in September to take part in one of the most challenging bike races: the Simpson Desert Bike Challenge – also called Five Days in Hell. The weather dependent race is physically and mentally exhausting.

You never know what's going to happen on the five day course. Track conditions vary greatly, with temperatures over 40°C, vast sand dunes covering the track and creeks holding water after heavy rainfalls make this race the toughest mountain bike endurance contest.

Being at the start line is the end of a preparation period of many months. The first obstacle is finding a driver and a vehicle. Then the packing needs all your attention. You need food and water supplies for ten days, camping gear and the bike with repair sets. Teams then can go on the three day drive to the desert settlement at Purni Bore, South Australia.

So why do some MTB riders return to this torture every year? It might be the challenge of obtaining the elusive 100% medaillon, or the expectation of stage wins, but the sharing of the same emotions and cameraderie are also reasons for taking part in the event. The race lasts five days. The total distance is about 590 km and is split up into four days with morning stages of around 80 km starting at 6 am and afternoon stages of about 50 km starting at 2 pm. On day five there's only one final morning stage finishing outside the Birdsville Hotel in Queensland. After the first day on the track riders get an idea about the brutality of the race. At the end of the stage some of them just drag their exhausted bodies over the finishing line ahead of the sweep. Riders must proceed with a minimum speed of 12 km/h. If they don't, they are caught by the sweep car that brings them to the next starting point. Those unfortunate riders receive a time penalty, but they can restart the next stage. Usually the second day is the toughest. The incredible heat as well as visibility reducing sand storms let riders drop like flies. In 2009, only seven of over 50 starters managed to get through the morning stage, the afternoon stage was completed by only one rider.

Day three and four are easier stages. The riders skirt around salt lakes and get plenty of opportunity to get off their bikes and admire the beautiful landscape while pushing the bike over the top of sand dunes. Drifts of sand up to one metre deep and many kilometres long make it hard to ride the bike. After bleak times of battling with sand storms and heavy sand tracks, the race finishes on the fifth day in a classic Australian spot: the Birdsville Hotel in the tiny outback town of Birdsville. There, charity auctions for the Royal Flying Doctor Service and other fund raising activities take place.

EXTRA: Creative writing

A. *Imagine you are a tiny mouse living in the desert. What do you think about the race?*

B. *If the bike could talk ... – what would it say?*

C. *Design a brochure about an MTB race in your area.*

35.2 An Australian bike challenge

Leseaufträge für die Gruppenarbeit:

A	B	C	D
Ask your group members questions that can be answered after reading the paragraph.	Give a summary of the paragraph. Your group members will tell you if it was well done. If not, they will correct wrong facts or add information.	Search for unknown words and phrases and explain them to your group.	Predict what is going to happen in the next paragraph.
A	B	C	D
Ask your group members questions that can be answered after reading the paragraph.	Give a summary of the paragraph. Your group members will tell you if it was well done. If not, they will correct wrong facts or add information.	Search for unknown words and phrases and explain them to your group.	Predict what is going to happen in the next paragraph.
A	B	C	D
Ask your group members questions that can be answered after reading the paragraph.	Give a summary of the paragraph. Your group members will tell you if it was well done. If not, they will correct wrong facts or add information.	Search for unknown words and phrases and explain them to your group.	Predict what is going to happen in the next paragraph.
A	B	C	D
Ask your group members questions that can be answered after reading the paragraph.	Give a summary of the paragraph. Your group members will tell you if it was well done. If not, they will correct wrong facts or add information.	Search for unknown words and phrases and explain them to your group.	Predict what is going to happen in the next paragraph.
A	B	C	D
Ask your group members questions that can be answered after reading the paragraph.	Give a summary of the paragraph. Your group members will tell you if it was well done. If not, they will correct wrong facts or add information.	Search for unknown words and phrases and explain them to your group.	Predict what is going to happen in the next paragraph.

Virtual water

Interesting facts about virtual water:

- The amount of water that is needed for growing plants and processing goods is called virtual water.

- The 'water footprint' of a country is defined as the amount of water needed for the production of goods and services consumed by the inhabitants of that country. In a globalized world this includes the use of global water resources, e.g. by importing high water consuming products (such as beef or cotton for example).

- The global average water footprint is found to be 1,240 m³/yr/cap. There are large differences between countries. In Germany the average water footprint is 1,545 m³/yr/cap.

- Today, cotton is the most important natural fibre used in the textile industries worldwide, amounting to 40% of the textile production. Any finished cotton product involves a chain of consequences on the water resources in the areas where cotton is grown and processed – mainly dry regions, e.g. in India and Uzbekistan. There are the effects of water depletion, i.e. using up water resources as well as the effects on water quality.

- Coffee is the most important agricultural product traded in the world and producing coffee requires a lot of water. Scientists found that for drinking one standard cup of coffee about 140 litres of water are needed. A standard cup of coffee is 125 ml. For example, to cover the total coffee consumption in the Netherlands 2.6 billion cubic metres of water are needed per year. The Dutch people account for 2.4% of the world coffee consumption. All together, the world population requires about 110 billion cubic metres of water per year in order to be able to drink coffee. This is equivalent to 1.5 times the annual Rhine runoff.

m³/yr/cap = cubic metre per year per capita *Kubikmeter pro Jahr und pro Kopf*

1. Working with the text

Read the text carefully. You may work with a partner. Use a dictionary for unknown words.

a) True or false?

  1. The water footprint is the amount of water needed for things people of a certain country use.
  2. There isn't a global average water footprint, because the countries are all different.

b) Make a mind map about 'virtual water'.

2. Make a guess!

Guess how much virtual water is hidden in the following things:

10 l – 13 l – 35 l – 140 l – 2,70 l – 4,200 l – 15,500 l

A German needs .... of virtual water every day.

A cup of coffee contains .... of virtual water, a cup of tea ....

.... are needed for a cotton T-shirt, ... for 1 kg beef.

There are .... in an A4 sheet of paper and .... in a 70 g tomato.

EXTRA

Work in groups and collect ideas on how you can save water in your everyday life. Also consider the impact of virtual water. Think about at home, at school, in your community.

1. Talking spices

a) Do you know these spices? Read the clues and fill in the right numbers.

(1) kurkuma

(2) fenugreek

(3) poppy seed

(4) star anise

(5) cinnamon

(6) lemongrass

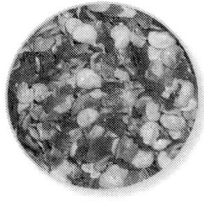
(7) chili

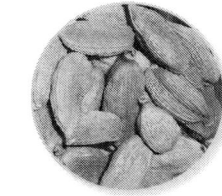
(8) cardamom

( ) I come from South East Asia. In Thailand many dishes are prepared with me. I can be used fresh or dried. I'm green and smell fresh like lemons, therefore I am refreshing and especially good when you feel a lack of concentration. Pour hot water over me and you have a fine tea or use me for marinating fish, chicken or meat.

( ) The region I grow in is Turkey, but I also like India. There are three different kinds of me: green, black and white and some people call me the Queen of spices. I have a pungent eucalyptus-like taste. I'm used as aroma in curries and chais (Indian milk teas), I promote digestion and make a fresh breath.

( ) I come from India. I'm used in chutneys and sauces. I taste bitter, like burnt sugar. I consist of thousands of little brown seeds. People think I can reduce fever, high blood pressure and stomach aches. I can even be used as a treatment for diabetes.

( ) I come from Africa, but you also find me in India. I'm quite tasteless but I have a deeply yellow colour. I'm part of a root. Therefore I'm used in curries. People believe that I am antiseptic and antibiotic.

( ) I am part of the bark of a tree. I grow in Indonesia, I'm brown and you can find me in desserts, pastries and teas. I'm sweet, fragrant and even pungent. I give you a warm feeling when you drink me in a tea. I work against colds and stimulate your blood circulation.

( ) I am hot, incredibly hot and pungent. I'm green or red. I'm small and look like a tiny bell pepper. My home is South America. I'm full of Vitamin C and I can work as a pain-relief. I'm also good in promoting your digestion.

( ) I come from India. I consist of thousands of little seeds in black or white. I'm very aromatic and nutty. I'm used in pastries and cakes and also to thicken curries.

( ) I look wonderful – like a star. My home is in Asia. You find me in drinks and confections. My taste is bitter-sweet, liquorice-like. I soothe your stomach and promote digestion.

Spice it up!

37.2

b) Read the clues again and fill in the table below.

no.	spice	region	taste – smell – colour – shape
1			
2			
3			
4			
5			
6			
7			
8			

2. Time to try Indian food

These two recipes are mixed up. Read them and find out what you need for a mango lassi and for Indian chicken. Put the recipes in the right order and write A or B with the numbers.

(A) Lassi – a typical Indian drink   **(B)** Indian chicken

○ ☐ You need 250 g yoghurt, 100 ml water, 150 g mango (cut into small pieces), 4 teaspoons sugar, 1 teaspoon lemon juice, some rose water, a pinch of cardamom.

○ ☐ Put in the yoghurt and add the water gradually. Cook for about 15 minutes. Serve with rice.

○ ☐ The beverage consists of fresh fruit and milk or yoghurt. Essential for lassi drinks are the spices that are added. Try this recipe:

○ ☐ Put in all the other ingredients and stir well. Decorate with daisies, mint or balm leaves.

○ ☐ Put the mango in a mixer and blend well with yoghurt and water.

○ ☐ Heat up oil and butter, put in cardamom then add the chicken breast and deep fry. Put in the other spices and tomatoes. Stir well.

○ ☐ You need 3 chicken breasts, cut into small pieces and salted, 5 tablespoons oil, 1 tablespoon butter, 1½ tablespoons cardamom, 1 tablespoon chili, 1 tablespoon kurkuma, 2 tablespoons canned tomatoes, 300 g yoghurt, 300 ml water, salt.

How polite are you? Test yourself.

a) *Read the questions and answers carefully. Then decide and tick (✓) your choice for the best answer.*

b) *Work with a partner. Compare your answers. Discuss why you think your choice is the most polite one.*

1. You want to spend a year abroad after school. You have to write an application for the organization you work with. How do you address people?
   - [ ] a) Hello!
   - [ ] b) Dear Sir or Madam
   - [ ] c) Dear all

2. You are taking part in a formal event. Is it OK to leave your hands in the pockets of your trousers/skirt/jacket?
   - [ ] a) Yes, it is. It looks cool and casual.
   - [ ] b) No, it isn't. It's impolite.
   - [ ] c) During longer talks it is OK to have one hand in a pocket. But it is impolite when you enter or leave the room.

3. You arrive late at the cinema, the film has already started. To get to your seat you …
   - [ ] a) climb over the seats.
   - [ ] b) go to your row, then you go to your seat with your back towards the screen.
   - [ ] c) go to your row, then you go to your seat with your back towards the people.

4. You are at a job interview. Your future boss sneezes.
   - [ ] a) You say "Bless you".
   - [ ] b) You ask, if he/she has caught a cold.
   - [ ] c) You ignore it.

5. You want to phone one of your classmates at home. To be polite you have to phone …
   - [ ] a) no later than 8 pm.
   - [ ] b) before 10 pm.
   - [ ] c) It is generally not polite to call a family in the evening.

6. During a work placement you are invited to a formal dinner. While speaking with your colleagues you talk …
   - [ ] a) only when you are asked.
   - [ ] b) about religion and politics.
   - [ ] c) about things you found interesting during your work placement.

7. You have a holiday job in an office and sometimes you have to answer the phone. What do you say?
   - [ ] a) The name of the company, your name and position, "good morning/afternoon".
   - [ ] b) Your name, "hello".
   - [ ] c) The name of the company and "good morning/afternoon".

8. You are planning to do a work placement in the office of the townhall. What about the dress code?
   - [ ] a) You are an individual and wear whatever you like.
   - [ ] b) You ask your friends.
   - [ ] c) You phone the townhall and ask what they expect you to wear.

EXTRA

A. *Choose one of the following situations and write a short text for a decent behaviour guidebook.*

B. *Choose one of the following situations and take notes about how you should / shouldn't behave.*

| **job interview:** greeting, introduction, dress code, body talk, eye contact, … | **first date:** greeting, who pays the bill?, (small) talk topics, dress code, … | **Internet platforms and social networks:** greeting unknown people, How much do I tell others about myself?, How do I communicate with strangers?, Do I trust everyone in the web?, … |

decent *proper, respectable* – **behaviour** *the way people behave*

Let's talk: On a class trip

A. At the reception of the youth hostel

You are on a class trip. After a long journey you have arrived safely at the youth hostel.
Act out the situation with a partner.

Receptionist	You
• Grüße und biete Hilfe an.	• Grüße und sage, dass ihr Zimmer für drei Nächte gebucht habt. Du gehörst zu der deutschen Klasse aus …
• Frage nach der Personenzahl.	• Sage, dass ihr 21 Schüler und zwei Lehrer seid.
• Sage, dass die Schüler in 3-Bett Zimmern untergebracht sind, die Lehrer jeweils ein Einzelzimmer haben.	• Sage, dass das super ist und erkundige dich, wo sich Toilette und Dusche befinden.
• Sage, dass sich Toiletten und Duschen auf der Etage befinden.	• Frage, wo es Frühstück gibt.
• Sage, dass es ab 7.00 Uhr Frühstück im großen Raum im dritten Stock gibt.	• Frage, ob es die Möglichkeit gibt, Lunchpakete zu bekommen und wo man abends Snacks und Getränke kaufen kann.
• Sage, dass Lunchpakete kein Problem sind, die Küche es nur am Abend vorher wissen muss. Getränke und Snacks kann man bis 22.00 Uhr an der Rezeption erwerben.	• Bedanke dich für die Auskunft.
• Überreiche die Zimmerschlüssel. Wünsche einen schönen Aufenthalt.	• Reagiere.

B. Lost and found

At the youth hostel you discover that you have lost your bag. Ask the receptionist for help.
Act out the situation with a partner.

Receptionist	You
• Grüße und biete Hilfe an.	
	• Grüße. Sage, dass du deine Tasche verloren hast. Du hast sie im Zug liegen lassen.
• Frage, in welchem Zug und erkundige dich nach dem Aussehen der Tasche.	
	• Nenne den Zug und beschreibe die Tasche.
• Erkundige dich nach dem Inhalt.	
	• Sage, was sich in der Tasche befindet.
• Nimm die Personalien auf, frage nach der Adresse für den Fall, dass die Tasche gefunden wird.	
	• Nenne deine Personalien.
• Sage, dass du alles notiert hast und du dich um das Problem kümmern wirst. Verabschiede dich.	
	• Reagiere.

Let's talk: On a class trip

C. At the boat rental

On a class trip you want to rent canoes for a trip down the river.
Act out the situation with a partner.

Canoe rental staff	You
• Begrüße den Kunden und biete deine Hilfe an.	
	• Grüße. Sage, dass du Boote für einen Ausflug mieten möchtest.
• Frage, welche Boote (Ruderboote oder Kanus) gemeint sind?	
	• Sage, dass du Kanus brauchst.
• Erkundige dich nach der Personenzahl, dem Alter der Schüler und dem Namen des Lehrers.	
	• Sage, dass ihr 21 Schüler im Alter von 16 Jahren seid und euer Lehrer Herr Martin heißt.
• Sage, dass die Klasse 8 Kanus braucht.	
	• Erkundige dich nach dem Preis und frage, ob ihr noch etwas anderes braucht.
• Sage, dass 24 Euro pro Tag und Kanu anfallen, Schwimmwesten und wasserdichte Tonnen sowie eine Karte mit Sehenswürdigkeiten dabei sind.	
	• Frage, ob ihr am Ende der Tour abgeholt werdet.
• Bejahe die Frage und erkläre, dass es gut wäre, wenn die Tour hier gegen 9 Uhr beginnen würde. Um 17 Uhr werdet ihr 12 km flussabwärts abgeholt.	
	• Frage nach, was mit den Booten ist.
• Erkläre, dass die Boote aus dem Wasser raus müssen und an den gekennzeichneten Stellen abgelegt werden.	
	• Bedanke und verabschiede dich.
• Reagiere.	

D. Shopping

After you've done a sight-seeing tour through the town you are allowed to spend two hours on your own.
You want to buy a pair of jeans. Act out the situation with a partner.

Shop assistant	You
• Grüße und biete Hilfe an.	• Grüße. Sage, dass du auf der Suche nach einer Jeans bist.
• Frage nach der Farbe.	• Sage, dass du eine dunklere bevorzugst, aber „used" soll sie aussehen.
• Frage, ob es eine bestimmte Marke sein soll, frage nach der Größe.	• Sage, dass die Marke keine Rolle spielt. Nenne deine Größe.
• Du bemerkst den deutschen Akzent. Erkundige dich nach der Herkunft des Kunden.	• Sage, dass du aus … in Deutschland kommst und mit deiner Klasse hier bist.
• Zeige dich begeistert und berichte, dass du da auch schon einmal warst. Empfiehl eine Hose. Verweise auf die Umkleidekabine. Erkundige dich, ob die Hose passt.	• Sage, dass die Hose zu groß ist und bitte um eine andere.
• Erkundige dich erneut nach der Passform.	• Sage, dass diese perfekt sitzt.
• Sage, dass die Hose wirklich gut passt. Frage, ob es noch ein passendes Oberteil dazu sein soll.	• Verneine. Frage nach dem Preis der Hose. Sage, dass du einen Gürtel möchtest.
• Nenne den Preis für Hose und Gürtel.	• Sage, dass du beides nimmst.
• Verweise auf die Kasse. Bedanke und verabschiede dich.	• Reagiere.

Let's talk: On a class trip

E. Medical help

You played volleyball all afternoon. In the last match the accident happened. The ball came, you jumped, got it right into the other team's field – but you hurt your foot. You cannot walk and have to see the doctor. Act out the situation with a partner.

Nurse	You
• Begrüßung. Frage, was los ist.	• Erwidere den Gruß. Sage, dass du beim Volleyball spielen umgeknickt bist und nun nicht mehr auftreten kannst.
• Erkläre, dass du zuerst die Personalien brauchst. Frage nach Namen, Adresse, Land sowie dem Aufenthaltsort hier.	• Nenne Namen, Adresse, Land und den Namen der Jugendherberge.
• Erkundige dich, wer für den Patienten verantwortlich ist.	• Nenne den Namen des Lehrers.
• Sage, dass der Patient dir ins Untersuchungszimmer folgen soll. Der Arzt wird sich gleich den Fuß anschauen.	
Doctor	
• Begrüßung. Schau dir den Fuß an und frage, was passiert ist.	• Erwidere den Gruß. Erkläre dem Arzt den Vorfall. Sage, was weh tut.
• Gib die Diagnose bekannt: Der Fuß ist verstaucht. Der Patient muss einen Verband kriegen, den Fuß kühlen und hochlegen. Beruhige den Patienten, indem du sagst, dass es nicht so schlimm ist.	• Sage, dass das gut klingt. Frage, ob du noch einmal zum Arzt kommen sollst.
• Erkläre: Wenn die Schmerzen weniger werden und du wieder auftreten kannst, dann nicht.	
• Nein, erkläre, dass das die Versicherung trägt.	• Frage, ob du etwas bezahlen musst.
• Wünsche noch einen angenehmen Aufenthalt.	• Bedanke und verabschiede dich.

food (1)	pasta bread sweets		**verbs (1)**	eat drink cook
food (2)	chocolate cake ice-cream fruit salad		**verbs (2)**	smell taste bake
food (3)	smoothies muesli whole meal bread		**adjectives**	delicious disgusting spicy
food (4)	lettuce walnuts tuna		**drinks**	Latte Macchiato soft drinks water
junk food	hot dog chips toasties		**dairy products**	cheese yoghurt buttermilk
eating out	fast food restaurant cafeteria snack bar		**meals**	brunch dinner breakfast
places	ice-cream shop soup kitchen take away		**jobs**	dinner lady waiter chef
fruits	strawberry pineapple orange		**spices**	basil cinnamon curry
vegetables	cauliflower cucumber tomato		**seasoning & spices**	salt pepper chili

Sport words – a guessing game

verbs (1)	surf / swim / dive	**warm-up exercises**	sit-ups / press-ups / pull-ups
verbs (2)	climb / hike / ride	**endurance sport**	inline skating / jogging / rowing
verbs (3)	jump / accelerate / throw	**tough games**	ice hockey / rugby / handball
verbs (4)	stretch / bend / hold	**competitions**	Olympic Games / championships / sports day
places (1)	fitness centre / gym / swimming pool	**body control**	juggling / unicycling / acrobatics
places (2)	mountains / sea / lake / forest	**water sports**	aquaball / canoeing / snorkeling
equipment (1)	bike / slackline / racket	**unusual sports**	elephant polo / shoe tossing / wok racing
equipment (2)	tennis ball / frisbee / net	**music**	cheerleading / aerobics / jazz dance
equipment (3)	skipping rope / parachute / helmet	**people**	couch potato / sports journalist / goalkeeper
kinds of sport	volleyball / chess / skiing	**injuries**	broken finger / strained ankle / laceration

How to play Jobtivity

You need: one die, counters (one per team), a stopwatch, chalk, board

The whole class participates in this game. Play in teams of three to four people. One player of each group rolls the die, the player with the highest number starts the game with his / her team. The player picks a card. In the first round he/she can act, draw or explain the word. In the following rounds, the player then has to pick the word that matches the symbol on the game board describe it accordingly.

 act out the job without saying anything

 draw clues for the job without saying anything

 explain the job without saying its name

The other team members have got one minute to guess the word. If they guess right, the team's counter moves forward the number of spaces given on the card. The team who first gets to the finishing line is the winner.

Jobtivity — 42.2

👤 – bricklayer ⚂	👤 – doctor ⚂	👤 – carpenter ⚂
✏️ – hairdresser ⚄	✏️ – nurse ⚄	✏️ – IT specialist ⚄
💬 – teacher ⚅	💬 – politician ⚅	💬 – baker ⚅

👤 – bishop ⚂	👤 – vet ⚂	👤 – fashion designer ⚄
✏️ – biologist ⚄	✏️ – plumber ⚄	✏️ – baby-sitter ⚂
💬 – shop assistant ⚅	💬 – artist ⚅	💬 – bank clerk ⚅

👤 – housewife ⚄	👤 – chef ⚄	👤 – secretary ⚄
✏️ – social worker ⚂	✏️ – TV cook ⚂	✏️ – butcher ⚂
💬 – clown ⚅	💬 – waiter/waitress ⚅	💬 – headteacher ⚅

👤 – electrician ⚄	👤 – lawyer ⚅	👤 – radio journalist ⚅
✏️ – roofer ⚂	✏️ – forester ⚄	✏️ – newsagent ⚄
💬 – beautician ⚅	💬 – TV journalist ⚂	💬 – interpreter ⚂

👤 – pilot ⚅	👤 – guide ⚅	👤 – zookeeper ⚅
✏️ – captain ⚄	✏️ – bodyguard ⚄	✏️ – blacksmith ⚄
💬 – fisherman ⚂	💬 – painter ⚂	💬 – farmer ⚂

👤 – bookseller ⚂	👤 – gardener ⚂	👤 – wine-grower ⚂
✏️ – librarian ⚄	✏️ – horse breeder ⚅	✏️ – laboratory assistant ⚄
💬 – receptionist ⚄	💬 – shepherd ⚄	💬 – engineer ⚄

– architect ⚂ – soldier ⚄ – press officer ⚃	– firefighter ⚂ – police officer ⚄ – physiotherapist ⚃	– restorer ⚃ – optician ⚂ – watchmaker ⚄
– flying instructor ⚃ – flight controller ⚂ – goldsmith ⚄	– art director ⚃ – newsreader ⚂ – software developer ⚄	– postman/postwoman ⚃ – graphic artist ⚂ – cartoonist ⚄
– dinner lady ⚃ – bus driver ⚂ – midwife ⚄	– camera operator ⚂ – script writer ⚃ – musician ⚄	– talk show host ⚂ – comedian ⚃ – hotel maid ⚄
– make-up artist ⚂ – disc jokey ⚄ – ticket collector ⚃	– factory worker ⚂ – (football) coach ⚄ – flight attendant ⚃	– actor ⚂ – receptionist ⚄ – driving instructor ⚃
– dance instructor ⚄ – dentist ⚃ – florist ⚂	– climbing instructor ⚄ – travel agent ⚃ – judge ⚂	– swimming instructor ⚄ – street sweeper ⚃ – web designer ⚂
– tailor ⚃ – security staff ⚂ – novelist ⚄	– conductor ⚃ – sound engineer ⚂ – sales representative ⚄	– ballet dancer ⚃ – riding instructor ⚂ – poet ⚄

Vertretungsstunden
Englisch Sek I
ISBN 978-3-12-927927-4

Dictionary skills: False friends

1. False friends

There are lots of false friends between English and German, i.e. English words that look or sound like a German word but have a completely different meaning. For example, the the German word "bekommen" means "get" in English.

When will I become a beefsteak?

I hope never.

a) Find the correct translation with the help of a dictionary.

German	English
Mappe	
Eintrittskarte	
aktuell	
sympathisch	
Bank	
bekommen	
eventuell	
Unternehmer	
Prospekt	
ordinär	
sensibel	

English	German
map	
(post)card	
actual	
sympathetic	
bank	
become	
eventual	
undertaker	
prospect	
ordinary	
sensible	

b) Choose the right word(s) according to the context.

1. On a hiking tour you need a **card / map / ticket / folder**.
2. At the cinema you buy a **card / map / ticket / folder**.
3. On your computer, you save documents in a **map / folder**.
4. You need a special lotion for **sensible / sensitive** skin.
5. Drinking and driving is definitely not a **sensible / sensitive** thing to do.
6. A company owner is an **undertaker / employer**.
7. Relax and have a rest on a **bank / bench** during lunch break.
8. **Eventually / Maybe** Nigel will go to Iceland in the summer holidays.
9. People who feel sorry for the fate of others are very **sympathetic / friendly**.
10. When will you **get / become** your new mobile phone?
11. Take a look at the **brochure / prospect / leaflet** to find out more about the hotel.
12. In the USA the name Joe Average is used to represent **ordinary / vulgar** people.

EXTRA

To help you not to confuse words, make some cue cards with definitions and phrases.

undertaker – employer   **bank – bench**   **ticket – card**   ...

44

Dictionary skills: Synonyms

1. Words with a similar meaning

A synonym is a word that has a similar meaning to another word. Find the synonyms for the words in the box. Draw lines. You can use a dictionary for help.

hard   purchase   fortunate   depart   amazed

| angry | difficult | careful | buy | leave | close | rude | lucky | persuade | surprised | find |

furious   near   convince   cautious   impolite   locate

2. Replace them!

Use the words from exercise 1 to replace the words written in bold.

1. Whenever I want to go out I can't **find** my mobile and my keys. ....
2. It's **rude** to arrive late at a birthday party. ....
3. Josh's parents **bought** a new house in our street. ....
4. The maths test was really **difficult**. Nigel only got 60 % right. ....
5. Pauline and Kate sat **close** to each other. ....
6. On a slippery surface, you must be very **careful**. ....
7. Alex was **angry** when his smart phone was stolen. ....
8. Teachers are often **surprised** by their students. ....
9. The plane is scheduled to **leave** at 10:47. ....
10. On the class trip to York, the students spent the nights in nice youth hostel. They were **lucky**, because there are also lots of run down places. ....
11. Annie loved the bungee jump, but she couldn't **persuade** her father to do one, too. ....

3. More synonyms

Look up the German meaning of the words in a dictionary. Then find a synonym for the word.

German	English synonyms	
	considerate	
	modern	
	committed	
	catastrophe	
	(to) annoy s.o.	
	trustworthy	
	playwright	

Kommentar mit Lösungen

Worksheet 1: The four seasons

Lernziele

- Lexik zum Thema Jahreszeiten trainieren
- Transferleistung: eigenes Gedicht oder eigene Geschichte schreiben

Material

- evtl. Lose zur Einteilung der Gruppen
- Wörterbücher
- Buntstifte zum Gestalten der Gedichte

Kommentar

Aufgabe 1:

Zur Einstimmung auf das Thema schreiben SuS die entsprechende Jahreszeit unter das Bild.

Aufgabe 2:

Einteilung der vier Gruppen: Dies kann auf verschiedene Weise geschehen:

a) SuS selbst wählen lassen

b) Entscheidung per Los (Nummern oder Jahreszeit oder für die Jahreszeit typische Bilder auf Kärtchen schreiben/drucken)

c) SuS stellen sich entsprechend ihrer Geburtstage in einer Reihe auf, LuL zählt ab und teilt in Gruppen auf

Es muss festgelegt werden, wer schreibt, wer präsentiert, wer die Zeit im Auge behält.
Die SuS bearbeiten die Aufgabe in ihrer Gruppe, sammeln Lexik in der Tabelle.
Nach zehn Minuten findet sich die Klasse im Plenum zusammen, die Gruppen stellen ihre Ergebnisse vor. Es kann zu Überschneidungen bei einigen Begriffen kommen. Es darf diskutiert werden!
Um einen Überblick über alle Jahreszeiten zu haben, können die SuS nun den Auftrag bekommen, sich zu den drei anderen Jahreszeiten Notizen zu machen, z. B. jeweils zwei Stichpunkte pro Kategorie.

Aufgabe 3:

Mit der nun bekannten Lexik schreiben die SuS ein Gedicht oder eine Geschichte. Sie können selbst entscheiden. Eine Differenzierung nach Arbeitstempo und Niveau ist möglich, da sich die SuS frei äußern oder sich an den vorgegebenen Texten entlang bewegen können *(scaffolding)*.
Ein Ausstellungsrundgang mit Vorstellung der eigenen Werke beendet die Stunde.

Lösungen

spring	summer	autumn	winter
warm, cloudy, windy	hot, sunny	stormy, chilly, foggy, rainy	cold, freezing
trainers, cap, fleece, jacket, long-sleeved shirt	sandals, T-shirt, shorts, bikini, blouse, dress, skirt, tank top	wellingtons, cap, pullover, rain jacket, trousers, cardigan, sweatshirt	boots, scarf, woollen hat, mittens, anorak, coat
cycling, running, playing football	swimming, playing volleyball, sun bathing, picking berries	flying a kite, hiking, playing outside, playing inside, picking mushrooms	skiing, ice-skating, going sledging, building a snowman, throwing snowballs, snowboarding, wearing costumes

*bei den Aktivitäten und Kleidungsstücken gibt es verschiedene Lösungen, z. B. kann man immer draußen und drinnen spielen, Kostüme trägt man an Fasching und an Halloween. Die SuS können im Plenum darüber sprechen.

Worksheet 2: All kinds of animals

Lernziel
Lexiktraining

Material
evtl. Wörterbücher für die Extra-Aufgaben

Kommentar

Aufgabe 1:

Als Warming-up schreiben die SuS zehn Tiere auf.
Diese Aufgabe kann in Einzel- oder in Partnerarbeit erledigt werden. Um die Wörter zu festigen und um sich das Schriftbild einzuprägen, bilden die SuS aus den Wörtern eine Wortschlange. Es dürfen neue Wörter hinzukommen.

Aufgabe 2:

In Partnerarbeit werden nun alle Tiere aus Aufgabe 1 in die Tabelle eingetragen, der Wortschatz wird umgewälzt. Weitere Tiere werden hinzugefügt.

Extra:

Das Aufgabenangebot beschäftigt lernstärkere SuS.
- *Play animal Bingo.* (Dazu halten LuL eine Liste von Tieren an der Tafel oder auf Folie fest; die SuS zeichnen 3x3 Bingo-Spielfelder auf Blätter und tragen ihre individuelle Auswahl von den vorgegebenen Tieren ein.)
- *Chain game: I went to the zoo and I saw ...*

Lösungen

Aufgabe 2: Vorschlag

water	wild	farm	pets	birds
fish	elephant	sheep	cat	parrot
whale	tiger	chicken	dog	budgy
seal	lion	cow	hamster	sea gull
shark	hippo	goat	mouse	eagle
crocodile	zebra	horse	budgy	dove
penguin	flamingo	goose	goldfish	swan/duck
polar bear	bear	rabbit	bunny/rabbit	flamingo

Extra:

Lösungshinweise zu *alphabet*: (Wörterbucharbeit)
ape, antilope, ant eater, baboon, chimpanzee, crocodile, dingo, elephant, eagle, flamingo, giraffe, gecko, gnu, hippo, hedgehog, iguana, jellyfish, kangaroo, lion, lizzard, monkey, nanny goat, opossum, panda, quoll *(Beutelmarder)*, rhinoceros, snake, tiger, (u), vulture, wolf, (x), yak, zebra

Worksheet 3: A pet mouse

Lernziele

- Textverstehen
- Lesestrategien üben
- einfache Sachverhalte begründen

Kommentar

Die SuS lesen den Text und bearbeiten die Aufgaben selbstständig, die Kontrolle erfolgt im Plenum.

Lösungen

a) 1F, 2F, 3T, 4T, 5F, 6T, 7F, 8T

b) Vorschläge
   good: not expensive, need little space, don't smell, housing and feeding is simple
   bad: awake at night, cage must be cleaned, fresh food and water daily

c) *I would(n't) like to have a mouse, because ...* – Satzanfang für lernschwache SuS an die Tafel schreiben.

Worksheet 4: My favourite animal

Lernziel
über das Lieblingstier erzählen können (schriftlich)

Kommentar
Als Warming-up machen die SuS sich zuerst Notizen über ihr Lieblingstier. Die beiden Texte werden im Anschluss gelesen und dienen als Modell. Den SuS sollte viel Zeit eingeräumt werden, einen eigenen Text zu produzieren und diesen für ihren *English folder* auf einer ansprechend gestalteten Seite aufzuschreiben. Am Ende der Stunde sollte den SuS die Möglichkeit gegeben werden, ihre Texte vorzustellen.

Extra: Vorschläge zu *animal films*
Finding Nemo (2003), Madagascar 1-3 (2005), Ice Age 1-3 (2002, 2005, 2009), March of the Penguins (2005), Happy Feet (2006), Over the Hedge (2006), Earth (documentary, 2007), Chicken Run (2000), Shaun the Sheep (2007), Fantastic Mr Fox (2009), The Conference of the Animals (2010), ...

Worksheet 5: Animal fun

Lernziel
Witze verstehen

Kommentar
Die SuS finden Antworten zu den Scherzfragen. Sie können dies allein oder in Partnerarbeit tun.

Lösungen

1. What animal never tells the truth?
   c. A lion.
2. Why did the grizzly bear catch a cold?
   d. Because he went outside on his bare feet.
3. Why did it take the elephant so long to get on the airplane?
   a. Because he had to check in his trunk.
4. Why did the frog say "meow"?
   e. He was learning a foreign language.
5. Where should you never take a dog?
   b. To the flea market.
6. How do cats buy things?
   h. From a catalogue!
7. What did the bee say to the flower?
   i. Hello honey!
8. Why are dogs such bad dancers?
   f. Because they have two left feet.
9. Why does everyone love cats?
   l. They're purr-fect!
10. What kind of pets lie around the house?
    g. Carpets!
11. How do you start a teddy bear race?
    m. Ready, teddy, go!
12. What's grey and goes round and round?
    j. An elephant in a washing machine!
13. What do you call an elephant that flies?
    k. A jumbo jet.

Worksheet 6: How healthy do they eat?

Lernziele

- Fragebildung üben
- Lexik zu Obst/Gemüse wiederholen
- über eigene Essgewohnheiten nachdenken

Kommentar

Aufgabe 1:

Die SuS tragen die fehlenden Vokale ein.

Aufgabe 2:

Die SuS bewegen sich durch den Raum und befragen andere. LuL achtet auf korrekte Fragestellung und Kurzantworten. Die SuS machen sich Notizen. Im Anschluss schreiben die SuS einen Bericht. Ein Satzmodell ist gegeben.

Lösungen

Aufgabe 1:

cucumber	oranges	strawberries
tomatoes	cherries	lettuce

Extra:

Mögliche Lösungen für Obst- und Gemüsealphabet:
aubergine, broccoli, beans, cabbage, cucumber, carrot, corn, cherry, dried fruit, daisy, dandelion, Durian fruit, eggplant (AE for aubergine), fruits, grapefruit, grapes, gourgette (BE), honey melon, iceberg lettuce, (j), kiwi, lemon, lime, lentils, lettuce, mango, melon, mushroom, nectarine, orange, potatoes, pear, peas, peach, (red, green, yellow) pepper, quinche *(Quitte)*, raspberries, strawberries, spinach, tomatoes, tangerine, turnip, (u), vegetables, watermelon, (x), yellow zucchini, yam, zucchini (AE)

Worksheet 7: Making plans for the weekend

Lernziele

- Sachtexte verstehen
- Informationen zu Edinburgh lesen
- Vorschläge machen
- Verabredungen treffen

Kommentar

Aufgabe 1+2:

Die SuS lesen verschiedene Texte über Dinge, die es in Edinburgh zu tun gibt sowie Steckbriefe von Kindern, die eine für sie ansprechende Freizeitaktivität suchen.

Aufgabe 3:

 a) Zwei SuS tragen den Dialog mit verteilten Rollen der Klasse vor. Anschließend kann der Dialog dann paarweise gelesen werden.

b) Die SuS gestalten selbst einen Dialog. Lernschwache SuS orientieren sich dabei an Aufgabe 3a), leistungsstarke SuS gestalten einen freien Dialog. Möglichst viele Paare sollten ihren Dialog im Plenum vorstellen.

Worksheet 8: Let's talk: Meeting a friend

Lernziel

Gespräche führen

Kommentar

Die SuS finden jeweils die richtige Antwort zum sinnvollen Fortführen des Dialogs heraus. Im Plenum werden die richtigen Lösungen genannt. Der Dialog kann laut gelesen werden.

Die SuS finden sich paarweise zusammen und erstellen einen Dialog zu einer der Extra-Aufgaben.

Kommentar mit Lösungen

Lösungen

1b, 2c, 3a, 4c, 5a, 6c, 7c

Worksheet 9: Let's talk: Meeting friends (role cards)

Lernziel

Gespräche führen

Kommentar

Die SuS erhalten ihre Rollenkärtchen und erarbeiten paarweise die Dialoge. Die Realisierung der Kommunikationsabsicht ist hier wichtiger als Fehlerfreiheit. Den SuS soll bewusst werden, dass es immer mehrere Varianten gibt, einen Gedanken auszudrücken. Für eine zielorientierte Kommunikation ist es in erster Linie wichtig, dass ihr Gegenüber sie verstehen kann – dazu können sie auch ganz einfache Sätze formulieren.

Es sollte ausreichend Zeit bleiben zum Vorstellen der Dialoge, wenn möglich sollten diese gespielt werden.

Worksheet 10: Let's read: Three students – who is who?

Lernziele

- Textverstehen
- logisches Denken trainieren

Kommentar

Die beiden Denksport-Aufgaben *(logic puzzles)* von **WS 10** und **WS 11** ermöglichen einen nach Niveau differenzierten Einsatz: Das einfachere **WS 10** mit den Austauschschülerinnen und das knifflige **WS 11** mit dem entlaufenen Krokodil. Es sollte hier den SuS überlassen werden, ob sie einzeln oder in Partnerarbeit knobeln.

Lösungen

Anmerkung: Man schaut die drei Mädchen an, d.h. rechts und links beziehen sich auf den Betrachter.

name	Pauline	Annabel	Emma
colour of dress	green	pink	orange
colour of rucksack	blue	black	yellow

Worksheet 11: Let's read: Strange neighbours – who is who?

Lernziele

- Textverstehen
- logisches Denken trainieren

Kommentar

Die beiden Denksport-Aufgaben *(logic puzzles)* von **WS 10** und **WS 11** ermöglichen einen nach Niveau differenzierten Einsatz: Das einfachere **WS 10** mit den Austauschschülerinnen und das knifflige **WS 11** mit dem entlaufenen Krokodil. Es sollte hier den SuS überlassen werden, ob sie einzeln oder mit Partner knobeln.

Alle Kategorien der Denksport-Aufgabe zu Neighbours sind zufällig nach Lexikkenntnissen der 5./6. Klasse gewählt, es werden keine Stereotypen oder Klischees dargestellt. Die „besonderen" Haustiere wurden gewählt, um nicht immer Hamster, Katze, Hund usw. zu strapazieren.

Lösungen

Anmerkung: Man schaut die Häuser an, d.h. rechts und links beziehen sich auf den Betrachter. Das Rätsel lässt sich mithilfe des Ausschlussverfahrens lösen, z. B.:

a) Wenn das rote Haus in der Mitte ist, das blaue das neben dem Schotten aus dem ersten Haus, dann können grün und weiß nur die Nr. 4 und 5 sein, da sie ja nebeneinander stehen. Außerdem ergibt sich daraus, dass Nr. 1 gelb sein muss, da es als einziges noch übrig ist.

b) Wenn derjenige, der den Pinguin besitzt, Badminton spielt und im blauen Haus wohnt, dann liebt er Kartoffeln, da Äpfel, Tomaten und Birnen schon vergeben sind und der Rugbyspieler Gurken liebt. Das Krokodil ist nicht in den Hinweisen enthalten, da es in der Arbeitsanweisung erwähnt wird.

(Es ist durchaus empfehlenswert, das Rätsel selbst zu lösen, bevor man es den SuS aushändigt, denn so kann man sie immer wieder auf die richtige Fährte bringen.)

House no.	1	2	3	4	5
Colour	yellow	blue	red	green	white
Nationality	Scottish	Polish	French	German	Italian
Food	tomatoes	potatoes	apples	pears	cucumbers
Animal	rabbit	penguin	bear	**crocodile**	wolf
Sport	volleyball	badminton	climbing	biking	rugby

Worksheet 12: Opposites – adjectives

Lernziel

Gegenteile finden und anwenden können

Material

Wörterbücher

Kommentar

Aufgabe 1:

Die SuS finden die Gegensatz-Paare.

Aufgabe 2:

Die SuS finden passend zum Kontext das entsprechende Adjektiv.

Aufgabe 3:

Die SuS finden fünf Adjektive (lernschwache SuS wählen Adjektive aus Aufgabe 1), tauschen Arbeitsblätter und ergänzen die Gegensätze. Danach schreiben sie Sätze mit den Wortpaaren analog zu Aufgabe 2.

Lösungen

Aufgabe 1:

1. Kasten: exciting – boring, light – dark, cheap – expensive, tiny – huge, safe – dangerous, nervous – calm, beautiful – ugly, lazy - busy
2. Kasten: difficult – easy, sunny – cloudy, slow – fast, early – late, clean – dirty, short – long, heavy – light, bad – good

Aufgabe 2:

1. nervous / calm
2. huge / tiny
3. light / dark
4. sunny / cloudy
5. early / late
6. heavy / light
7. short / long
8. dirty / clean
9. dangerous / safe
10. fast / slow

Worksheet 13: Opposites – Pictionary

Lernziel

Gegenteile (Adjektiv Wortpaare) kennen und anwenden/erklären können

Material

- Schere
- Stoppuhr

Kommentar

LuL schneidet vorab die Karten aus. Die Karten werden verdeckt auf einen Stapel gelegt. Die Klasse wird in zwei Gruppen geteilt, jede Gruppe kann sich einen Namen geben, der dann an die Tafel geschrieben wird, um den Punktestand zu notieren. Ein SuS aus Gruppe A zieht nun eine Karte. Sie/er hat eine Minute Zeit, das Adjektivpaar zeichnerisch so darzustellen, dass ihre/seine Gruppe es erraten kann.

Worksheet 14: A crossword puzzle (relative clauses)

Lernziele

- Relativsätze üben
- Paraphrasieren üben

Kommentar

Relativsätze sind ein wichtiges Redemittel, um Begriffe zu paraphrasieren. In Aufgabe 1 lösen die SuS in Einzelarbeit das Kreuzworträtsel. Die sich daran anschließende Aufgabe 2 verlangt von den SuS, selbst Begriffe zu umschreiben und einen Partner raten zu lassen, worum es sich handelt.

Lösungen

1. pen
2. dictionary
3. enemy
4. detective
5. pizza
6. elephant
7. trumpet
8. computer
9. Vikings
10. queen

Worksheet 15: Dictionary skills: All in alphabetical order

Lernziel

Umgang mit dem Wörterbuch trainieren

Material

Wörterbücher

Kommentar

Die SuS bearbeiten das Worksheet in Einzelarbeit. Die Lösungen können im Plenum besprochen werden. Wichtig ist hier, dass die SuS ausreichend Zeit haben, um das Nachschlagen zu üben.

Aufgabe 1:

Die SuS schreiben acht Lieblingstiere auf und ordnen diese dann alphabetisch. Sie müssen die Wörter also zweimal schreiben, dies dient der Festigung der Schreibweise.

Aufgabe 2:

Die SuS bringen die Buchstaben in alphabetische Reihenfolge.

Aufgabe 3 + 4:

Die SuS ordnen Wörter nach dem Alphabet. In Aufgabe 3 nummerieren sie die Wortliste, in Aufgabe 4 werden die rechts stehenden Wörter per Pfeil in die Wortliste eingetragen. Beide Aufgaben erfordern eine hohe Konzentrationsleistung.

Aufgabe 5:

Leistungsstarke SuS können versuchen, anhand der Lautschrift die Wörter zu finden.

Lösungen

Aufgabe 2:

A – B – E – F – G – J – L – M – O – S – U – Y

Aufgabe 3:

1 interest – 2 interesting – 3 international – 4 interview – 5 invent – 6 invite – 7 island

Aufgabe 4:

beach – **beat** – beautiful – beauty – beaver – **become** – **bedroom** – bee – **begin** – behaviour – **behind** – bell – **belly** – belly button

Aufgabe 5:

school – freeze – clean – lunch – scary

Worksheet 16: Verbs, verbs, verbs (dictionary skills)

Lernziele

Umgang mit dem Wörterbuch trainieren

Material

Wörterbücher

Kommentar

Aufgabe 1:

Die SuS schlagen die Verben im Wörterbuch nach und schreiben diese auf.

Aufgabe 2:

Die SuS suchen die englischen Verben im Buchstabenraster (*wordsearch*).

Aufgabe 3:

Die SuS finden das passende Verb für die Phrase.

Lösungen

Aufgabe 1:

1. *gehen* – go
2. *fühlen* – feel
3. *machen* (2) – make, do
4. *sich unterhalten* (2) – talk, chat
5. *schwimmen* – swim
6. *sprechen* – speak
7. *nehmen* – take
8. *zuhören* – listen
9. *schreiben* – write
10. *geben* – give
11. *spielen* – play
12. *bezahlen* – pay
13. *überraschen* – surprise
14. *flüstern* – whisper

Aufgabe 2: Wordsearch

A	E	**M**	X	V	F	O	J	M	P	**G**	K	T	**P**	L
X	K	**A**	J	F	I	P	L	K	X	**I**	A	E	**L**	O
C	E	**K**	I	C	X	V	H	T	Q	**V**	K	**P**	**A**	Y
V	R	**E**	K	W	G	U	E	**L**	**E**	**F**	N	**Y**	D
M	W	O	**W**	**H**	**I**	**S**	**P**	**E**	**R**	J	A	H	I	G
N	Q	D	R	**G**	**O**	I	D	G	L	U	P	F	D	A
Z	**E**	T	O	J	L	K	A	S	**E**	M	N	E	V	**E**
U	**T**	G	A	S	W	D	U	**K**	B	V	E	R	**S**	C
O	**I**	B	C	X	R	J	**A**	Y	G	A	V	**I**	O	R
S	**R**	A	N	Q	G	**T**	H	Z	V	Z	**R**	H	A	M
S	**W**	I	M	D	S	Y	B	M	E	**P**	Y	A	Z	P
P	S	E	R	A	M	A	S	Y	**R**	U	A	T	K	I
E	W	I	P	**T**	**K**	D	E	**U**	D	A	E	L	S	S
A	R	H	**A**	**Z**	**L**	**I**	**S**	**T**	**E**	**N**	L	R	I	D
K	F	**H**	Y	E	**A**	A	G	W	H	E	E	P	**O**	Q
S	**C**	K	M	F	**T**	G	Z	A	J	S	U	P	U	**D**

Aufgabe 3:

1. do the homework
2. talk to strangers in a chatroom
3. swim in the lake every afternoon
4. go swimming
5. feel the cold breeze in the face
6. give the patient some medicine
7. play volleyball once a week
8. speak slowly, so that I can understand you
9. write a story about a castle
10. pay at the cash desk
11. whisper a secret to your friend
12. surprise your mum on her birthday
13. listen to your favourite songs
14. take the bus
15. make a cake

Worksheet 17: Irregular verbs – a maze

Lernziel

unregelmäßige Verben üben

Material

- Wörterbücher oder Liste unregelmäßiger Verben im Schülerbuch des Lehrwerks
- evtl. **WS 17** auf Folie kopiert

Kommentar

Aufgabe 1:

Die SuS finden ihren Weg durch das Labyrinth (*maze*). Der Weg geht vom Infinitiv zu den zwei anderen unregelmäßigen Formen und von da zum nächsten Infinitiv eines unregelmäßigen Verbs.
Zum Kontrollieren bietet es sich an, das *maze* auf Folie zu kopieren oder es an die verdeckte Tafel zu hängen. Dann können die SuS selbstständig eine Kontrolle durchführen.

Aufgabe 2:

Die SuS füllen die Tabelle mit den Verbformen aus dem *maze* aus.

Extra:

Mithilfe von Bewegung und Rhythmus werden die Verben gefestigt. Man kann eine Proberunde im Plenum durchführen, um den Rhythmus zu finden und dazu passend zu sprechen. Danach arbeiten die SuS mit einem Partner.

Erweiterung – zum Üben der *irregular verbs*:

Alle Verbformen stehen einzeln auf A4-Blättern. Exemplarisch legt LuL *be* in die eine Ecke des Zimmers, *was/were* in eine andere, *been* in die dritte Ecke. Jede/r SuS nimmt nun ein Blatt und legt es in die „richtige" Ecke.

be – think – feel – make – take – eat – find – let – wake – get – come – go – see

Lösungen

Augabe 1:

go, went, gone – wake, woke, woken – feel, felt, felt – take, took, taken – eat, ate, eaten – think, thought, thought – find, found, found – make, made, made – see, saw, seen

Worksheet 18: Once upon a time (irregular verbs)

Lernziele

- *simple past* Formen unregelmäßiger Verben üben
- fehlerfreies Abschreiben üben

Kommentar

Aufgabe 1:

Die SuS lesen das Märchen und ergänzen – mithilfe ihrer Kenntnis der Geschichte – die fehlenden Verbformen im *simple past*.

Aufgabe 3:

Die SuS lesen den Text komplett, danach satz- und phrasenweise in ihrem eigenen Tempo. Aus dem Gedächtnis schreiben sie das Märchen nach und nach ab.
Hier wird dem reproduktiven Schreiben bewusst Platz eingeräumt. Es ist kein mechanisch stupider Vorgang. Die SuS trainieren genaues und differenziertes Wahrnehmen. Korrektes Schreiben hat seine Bedeutung und kommt im Unterrichtsalltag zu kurz. In einer Vertretungsstunde bietet es sich deshalb an, das Abschreiben zu üben.

Lösungen

Once upon a time there **was** a Queen who **thought** Snow White **was** the most beautiful princess. She **went** to her house with a poisoned apple. When Snow White **ate** the apple, she **fell** asleep. The seven dwarves **were** very sad when they **found** her because they **thought** she **was** dead. They **made** a glass coffin and when a prince **came** by and **saw** her he **fell** in love with her. When the dwarves **took** the coffin to the castle they almost **let** it fall and then Snow White **woke** up again, spitting out the piece of poisoned apple. Soon after that, the prince and Snow White **got** married.

Worksheet 19: Feelings and moods

Lernziele

- Wortschatztraining Gefühle/Stimmungen
- über Gefühle sprechen

Kommentar
Aufgabe 1:

Die SuS ordnen den Gesichtern das entsprechende Adjektiv zu, indem sie es unter das jeweilige Bild schreiben. Da die Zuordnung aufgrund der Bedeutungsnuancen (z. B. zwischen *angry* und *annoyed*) nicht immer eindeutig ist, können die SuS ihre Wahl diskutieren und ggf. weitere Adjektive ergänzen.

Aufgabe 2:

Die SuS verwenden die Wörter aus Aufgabe 1 und schreiben in Einzelarbeit mindestens drei Sätze. Sie erklären, wie sie sich bestimmten Situationen fühlen. In einem nterrichtsgespräch werden noch einmal verschiedene Situationen angesprochen und das entsprechende Gefühl dazu benannt. In leistungsstarken Klassen können LuL weitere Adjektive vorgeben (excited, curious, exhausted, sleepy, frustrated, etc), die SuS bilden dann spontan Sätze nach dem eingeübten Muster.

Aufgabe 3:

Vier bis fünf SuS arbeiten in einer Gruppe. Der/Die Älteste der Gruppe beginnt und sucht sich ein Adjektiv aus Aufgabe 1 sowie einen Satz aus Aufgabe 3. Dieser Satz wird dann in der entsprechenden Stimmung vorgetragen. Was gesagt wird, ist weniger wichtig als die Gefühlslage die ausgedrückt wird. Die SuS dürfen nur Stimme und Mimik einsetzen, jedoch nicht die Hände. Funktioniert das nicht, müssen sich alle beim Sprechen auf die Hände setzen. Der gesagte Satz darf nur einmal wiederholt werden.

Lösungen
Aufgabe 1:

shy – relaxed – sad – friendly – bored – amazed
silly – angry – absent-minded – thoughtful – in love – frightened
indifferent – encouraging – cheeky – annoyed – content – tired

Worksheet 20: Mood-o-Meter

Lernziel

Gefühle ausdrücken

Material

- Scheren
- Verschlussklammern
- Farbstifte, <u>festeres</u> Papier zum Kopieren von **WS 20** (ggf. auf DIN-A3 vergrößert) verwenden
- Faden oder doppelseitiges Klebeband

Kommentar

Bevor es ans Basteln des „Mood-o-Meter" geht, sammeln die SuS in Einzel- oder Partnerarbeit Sätze, die verschiedene Gefühlslagen zum Ausdruck bringen. Anschließend wählen die SuS individuell Sätze aus und schreiben sie in Einzelarbeit auf jeweils ein Segment der Scheibe. Die SuS sollten dazu angehalten werden, so zu schreiben, dass das fertige „Mood-o-Meter" schön anzusehen ist.
(Wer z. B. gute Graffiti schreibt, kann hier gestalterisch arbeiten.) Die Deckblatt-Scheibe kann nach Belieben gestaltet werden.Das „Mood-o-Meter" kann zu Hause an die Zimmertür gehängt werden, sodass Eintretende sofort wissen, wie sich der/die Jugendliche fühlt.

Lösungshinweise

Weitere mögliche Sätze, z. B.:
- I'm tired. Please leave me alone.
- I'm in love. None of your business.
- I'm mad at you. Keep out for your own safety!

Worksheet 21: Your eating habits

Lernziele

- Über Essgewohnheiten nachdenken und sprechen
- Wortschatztraining Nahrungsmittel

Kommentar

Aufgabe 1:

Hier geht es darum, die Nahrungsmittel oder Gerichte in die Tabelle einzutragen. Dies geschieht in Einzelarbeit. Es gibt kein richtig oder falsch. Die Kategorien sind bewusst so gewählt, dass auch Mehrfachnennungen möglich sind. Was lecker ist, kann ebenfalls gesund sein – oder eben auch nicht. Was gesund ist, muss man nicht unbedingt mögen. Es gibt kein „unhealthy", stattdessen „packed with calories", um den SuS vor Augen zu führen, welche Nahrungsmittel kalorienreich sind und damit nur in Maßen verzehrt werden sollten. Darüber hinaus können die SuS die Tabelle ergänzen.

Aufgabe 2:

Hier werden die persönlichen Essgewohnheiten unter die Lupe genommen. Bei a) schreiben die SuS auf, was sie an einem normalen Tag zu den einzelnen Mahlzeiten zu sich nehmen. Bei b) reflektieren sie ihr Essverhalten mit den Erkenntnissen aus der Tabelle von Aufgabe 1. Sie können nun (für sie umsetzbare) Vorschläge für Änderungen ihres Essverhaltens in einer anderen Farbe hinzufügen. Bei c) zeigen sie ihre Aufzeichnungen einem Partner, der sich alles durchliest und Ratschläge zur Ernährung gibt. Danach werden die Rollen getauscht.

Worksheet 22: Jamie Oliver: "Feed Me Better"

Lernziele

- Lesekompetenz trainieren
- Interkulturelle Vergleiche bzgl. des Schulessens anstellen
- Meinungsäußerungen formulieren / Stellung nehmen

Kommentar

Aufgabe 1:

Die SuS bearbeiten Aufgabe 1 in Einzelarbeit. Bevor sie mit dem Lesen beginnen, kann der Text von LuL oder SuS vorgelesen werden, um auch über das Hören den Text zu erschließen. Die SuS sollten danach angehalten werden, den Text einmal komplett durchzulesen, bevor sie sich den Leseverstehensaufgaben zuwenden. Die SuS sollten auf *scanning techniques* hingewiesen werden.
Die Kontrolle erfolgt im Plenum.

Aufgabe 2:

Hier erklären die SuS den Begriff *junk food* mit eigenen Worten. Die Kontrolle erfolgt ebenfalls im Plenum. Bei weit auseinander liegenden Definitionen kann darüber diskutiert werden.

Aufgabe 3:

In Einzelarbeit schreiben die SuS einen Text zu einem der beiden Themen. Diese Arbeiten können im Anschluss vorgelesen und besprochen werden.

Extra:

Die Aufgaben A-C bieten weitere Schreibanlässe zum Thema.

Lösungen

Aufgabe 1:

1. true – 2. true – 3. true – 4. true – 5. false – 6. false – 7. true – 8. true

Aufgabe 2:

Mögliche Lösung:
Junk food is unhealthy food like sweets, chocolate bars, crisps and fizzy drinks. Junk food contains a lot of fat, salt and/or sugar.

Worksheet 23: A map of Scotland

Lernziele

- Texte verstehen
- Orte anhand von Hinweisen aus den Texten in eine Karte eintragen

Kommentar:

Die SuS beschäftigen sich in Einzelarbeit mit dem Worksheet. Sie lesen die Texte und finden anhand der *clues* heraus, an welcher Stelle in der Karte die Orte einzutragen sind. Die Kontrolle erfolgt im Plenum.

Extra:

Zusätzlich können die SuS eine der beiden Aufgaben wählen und in Partnerarbeit bearbeiten. Entweder schreiben sie Sätze über Schottland, die der Partner als richtig oder falsch erkennen muss oder sie denken sich Quizfragen aus, die der Partner beantwortet.

Lösung:

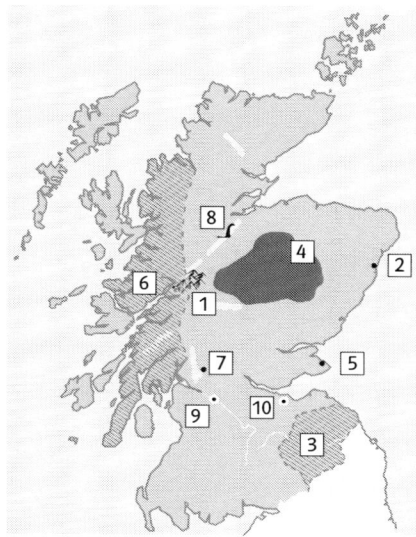

Worksheet 24: Group puzzle: Very Scottish

Lernziele

- Texte durch kooperative Verfahren verstehen
- landeskundliches Wissen sammeln

Material

Wörterbücher

Kommentar:

Die SuS arbeiten zu viert in Gruppen. Die Lesetexte werden als *group puzzle* bearbeitet.
Bevor die Arbeit los geht, notieren sich alle die folgenden Aufgaben ins Heft:
- What is the topic?
- What is interesting for you? (five facts)
- Discuss the interesting facts in your group.

Die Texte können mithilfe von zwei Verfahren bearbeitet werden:
1. In jeder Vierer-Gruppe wählt jeder SuS einen der vier Texte (ggf. per Zufallsverfahren). In Stillarbeit lesen die SuS ihre Texte und machen sich Notizen zu den Aufgaben. Im Anschluss stellen sie ihren Text der Gruppe in einem Kurzvortrag vor. Die Gruppe hat Gelegenheit, um Rückfragen zu stellen.

2. In der Klasse gibt es vier (acht) Expertengruppen, die jeweils einen Text bearbeiten. Die SuS tauschen sich innerhalb ihrer Gruppe zu dem Text aus, klären Unklarheiten, markieren Fakten und verständigen sich über die wichtigsten/interessantesten Informationen aus dem Text.

Kommentar mit Lösungen

Im Anschluss werden in der Klasse neue Vierer-Gruppen zusammengestellt, sodass in jeder Gruppe ein Experte zu einem der vier Texte vertreten ist. Reihum präsentieren die SuS die Themen und geben Auskunft zu den fünf Fakten.
Die anderen SuS machen sich Notizen.

Worksheet 25: Blackfeet Nation

Lernziele

- Texte durch kooperative Verfahren verstehen
- Informationen zu den Blackfeet Indianern sammeln
- Interkulturelle Kompetenz erlangen

Material

- Wörterbücher
- Folie

Kommentar:

Um die Texte erschließen zu können, bilden die SuS Gruppen von je vier Personen.

LuL stellen das Leseverfahren in vier Schritten vor:

Choose one text about certain aspects of the life of Blackfeet Indians today. Form a group with other pupils who have chosen the same text.
1. Start with the photo and the headline. What do you think the text is about? Discuss.
2. Read the text closely.
3. In your group, help each other to understand the text. Clarify words and phrases you don't understand.
4. Discuss the text in your group. What was interesting for you? Prepare a short presentation of the text.

Dann präsentiert jede Gruppe im Plenum – auf Folie werden Informationen über die Blackfeet Indianer festgehalten, sodass am Ende eine Art *fact sheet* entsteht.

Zusätzliche Aufgaben:

Die SuS recherchieren im Internet zur Blackfeet Nation und erweitern so ihr Wissen über die Texte hinaus. Im Sinne des interkulturellen Lernens können die SuS im Anschluss einen interkulturellen Vergleich anstellen: Are there any traditions in your area? Describe them.

Worksheet 26: Crazy sports

Lernziele

- Leseverstehen trainieren
- Über Attraktivität und Gefahren von *crazy sports* sprechen

Kommentar

Aufgabe 1:

Die SuS lesen die Definitionen und ordnen diesen die Sportarten zu. Dies geschieht in Einzelarbeit. Im Anschluss diskutieren die SuS die Sportarten im Hinblick auf Attraktivität, Gefahren, etc. im Plenum.

Lösung:

Aufgabe 1:

A 3 – B 4 – C 9 – D 5 – E 1 – F 7 – G 2 – H 6 – I 8

Kommentar mit Lösungen

Worksheet 27: Let's talk! A bike trip

Lernziel

Schulung der kommunikativen Kompetenz

Kommentar

WS 27.1 – 27.3 bietet drei mal zwei *role cards* mit kommunikativen Situationen (A, B, C), die mit dem Kontext einer Klassenfahrt nach England durchaus der Lebenswirklichkeit der SuS entsprechen.
Die SuS suchen sich eine der Situationen aus und erarbeiten mithilfe der *role cards* paarweise die Dialoge (in realen Situationen sind die SuS aus Sicherheitsgründen wohl immer in Paaren unterwegs).

Da nicht alle SuS alle drei *role cards* gleichzeitig brauchen, kann die Anzahl der Kopien niedrig gehalten werden.

Die Realisierung der Kommunikationsabsicht ist hier wichtiger als Fehlerfreiheit. Den SuS soll bewusst werden, dass es immer mehrere Varianten gibt, einen Gedanken auszudrücken. Für eine zielorientierte Kommunikation ist es in erster Linie wichtig, dass ihr Gegenüber sie verstehen kann – dazu können sie auch ganz einfache Sätze formulieren. Es sollte ausreichend Zeit bleiben zum Vorstellen der Dialoge, wenn möglich sollten diese gespielt werden.

Worksheet 28: In other words

Lernziele

- Umgang mit dem Wörterbuch trainieren
- ein Wortfeld kennen und nutzen lernen

Material

Wörterbücher

Kommentar

Aufgabe 1:

Die SuS beschäftigen sich mit dem Wortfeld gehen. Sie ordnen die deutschen Wörter den englischen zu, dabei können sie das Wörterbuch benutzen. Im Anschluss daran wenden sie die Wörter im Kontext an. Die Aufgabe kann in Einzel- oder Partnerarbeit erledigt werden.

Aufgabe 2:

Die SuS identifizieren das Wort, das nicht in die jeweilige Reihe passt, the *odd word*.
Die Kontrolle erfolgt im Plenum. Evtl. müssen einige Begriffe auch nachgeschlagen werden, z. B. *trip over, race*.

Mögliche Erweiterung:
Die SuS suchen mithilfe von Wörterbüchern weitere Verben zum Wortfeld gehen, z. B. bummeln – dawdle; schwanken – stagger; schleichen – creep, tiptoe; vorbeilaufen – pass; etc

Lösung

Aufgabe 1:

a) crawl – krabbeln, escape – entkommen, hike – wandern, hurry – eilen, limp – humpeln, shuffle – schlurfen, stalk – sich anpirschen, anschleichen, stroll – bummeln, tramp – stapfen, walk – gehen

b) 1. hurry – 2. stroll – 3. escape – 4. tramp – 5. stalk – 6. limp – 7. walk – 8. shuffle – 9. crawl – 10. hike

Aufgabe 2:

1. hurry – run – race – **stroll**
2. stalk – **hurry** – stroll – crawl
3. **hike** – limp – shuffle – trip over
4. shuffle – tramp – stalk – **walk**

Worksheet 29: Adjectives and their opposites

Lernziel

Adjektive und ihre Gegenteile kennen

Material

Wörterbücher

Kommentar

Aufgabe 1:

Die SuS suchen die Gegenteile, die in Spiegelschrift in der Box abgedruckt sind. Für einige Adjektive sind dort zwei mögliche Lösungen angegeben, z. B. *great, fantastic*. Die Aufgabe wird in Einzelarbeit erledigt.

Aufgabe 2:

Die SuS suchen mithilfe des Wörterbuchs Gegenteile, die mit einem Präfix gebildet werden.

Aufgabe 3:

Die SuS suchen sieben Adjektive und notieren diese auf einem Blatt. Im Heft notieren sie die dazugehörigen Gegenteile. Hat ein SuS sieben Adjektive aufgeschrieben, geht er/sie an einen bestimmten Platz im Klassenzimmer und wartet dort auf den nächsten/die nächste mit vollständiger Adjektivliste. Die beiden tauschen dann ihre Listen und suchen nach den Gegenteilen. Im Anschluss erfolgt die Kontrolle in Partnerarbeit.

Lösung

Aufgabe 1:

1. active – lazy
2. alive – dead
3. ancient – modern
4. awful – great, fantastic
5. best – worst
6. calm – nervous, hyper
7. fabulous – terrible, awful
8. final – first
9. careful – careless
10. loud – quiet
11. optimistic – pessimistic
12. poor – rich
13. private – public
14. useful – useless

Aufgabe 2:

possible – impossible
polite – impolite
friendly – unfriendly
legal – illegal
natural – unnatural
real – unreal
spectacular – unspectacular
successful – unsuccessful
active – inactive
acceptable – unacceptable

Worksheet 30: Jeopardy game: All about adjectives

Lernziel

Synonyme und Antonyme trainieren

Material

- Spielplan (**WS 30.1**) auf Folie kopiert
- Ein bis zwei Kopien von **WS 30.2** für Spielleiter
- Stoppuhr

Kommentar:

Es werden zwei Spielleiter, die gut lesen können, gewählt. Diese erhalten den Spielplan mit Lösungen (**WS 30.2**). Die SuS teilen sich in zwei Teams auf. Ein Team beginnt und wählt eine Kategorie und eine Zahl. Nachdem der Spielleiter die Frage gestellt und die Multiple-Choice Lösungen gelesen hat, hat das Team eine Minute Zeit, sich für eine Antwort zu entscheiden. Der zweite Spielleiter ist der Zeitwächter mit Stoppuhr. Hat das Team die richtige Lösung gefunden, werden die gewonnen Punkte (10, 20, 30, 40 oder 50, je nach Zahl auf dem Spielplan) von einem Spielleiter notiert und das Team darf noch mal spielen. Ist die Lösung nicht richtig, ist das andere Team an der Reihe. Gleiches gilt, wenn die Zeit abgelaufen ist und keine Entscheidung getroffen wurde.

In der Kategorie *prefixes/suffixes* werden den SuS Wörter präsentiert, die es gar nicht gibt (z. B. *inhappy*). Das Spiel ist aber nur spielbar, wenn man auf eben diese Wortbildungen zurückgreift. Möchte man den SuS keine „falschen" Wörter zeigen, lässt man diese Kategorie weg.

Lösungen:

Die Lösungen sind auf **WS 30.2** für den Spielleiter fett gedruckt.

Worksheet 31: Dictionary skills: Look it up!

Lernziel

Umgang mit dem Wörterbuch trainieren

Material

Wörterbücher

Kommentar

Je nach Klassensituation ist es den SuS überlassen, das Worksheet in Einzel- oder Partnerarbeit zu bearbeiten. Die Kontrolle der Aufgaben erfolgt im Plenum.

Aufgabe 1:

Die SuS ordnen die Wörter in alphabetischer Reihenfolge.

Aufgabe 2:

Die SuS unterstreichen die betonte Silbe. Um diese zu finden, müssen sie die Lautschrift mit ihrer Symbolik verstehen.

Aufgabe 3:

Die SuS werden für die *false friends*-Problematik sensibilisiert. Mithilfe des Wörterbuchs schlagen sie die vorgegebenen Begriffe nach.

Aufgabe 4:

Die SuS bemerken, dass einige Wörter nicht der „normalen" Pluralbildung folgen, es aber durchaus auch eine Regelmäßigkeit für die auf „-f" endenden Wörter gibt, für andere dagegen nicht. Hinweis: Der reguläre Plural für *person* lautet *people*. Bei formalen Ausdrücken findet man aber auch den Plural *persons*, z. B. spricht man bei der Polizei von *missing persons*.

Lösungen

Aufgabe 1:

reassure – reboot – receiver – recent – reception – recipient – recognizable – recognize – recollect – recommend – recreational – rectangular – recycle

Aufgabe 2:

responsibility – naturally – international – interesting – handkerchief – fortunately – endanger – embarrassed – successful – impossible – energy – disposable

Aufgabe 3:

1. stool – *Hocker*
2. strand – *stranden, Faden, Strähne*
3. recipe – *Kochrezept*
4. (to) reclaim – *beanspruchen*
5. tramp – *Vagabund*
6. taste – *Geschmack, schmecken*
7. brave – *mutig*

A. Stuhl – *chair*
B. Strand – *beach*
C. Rezept – *prescription*
D. reklamieren – *to make a complaint*
E. Tramper – *hitchhiker*
F. Taste – *key*
G. brav – *good, well-behaved*

Aufgabe 4:

1. shelf – shelves; 2. person – people; 3. wolf – wolves; 4. child – children;
5. knife – knives; 6. mouse – mice

Worksheet 32: Dictionary skills: Finding words quickly

Lernziel

sicher mit dem Wörterbuch umgehen können

Material

Wörterbücher

Kommentar

Aufgabe 1:

Die SuS ordnen in Einzelarbeit die Wörter in alphabetischer Reihenfolge. Dabei können sie auch mit einem Partner in Wettstreit treten, um zu sehen, wer am Schnellsten ist.

Aufgabe 2:

Die SuS finden anhand des Alphabets heraus, welche der angegebenen Wörter der Liste zwischen den vorgegebenen *headwords* stehen. Diese Aufgabe bezieht sich nicht auf ein bestimmtes Wörterbuch, sondern übt die Fertigkeit, sich schnell und zielgerichtet in einem Wörterbuch zu orientieren.
Die Aufgabe lässt sich erweitern, indem LuL zu den in der Klasse vorhandenen Wörterbüchern weitere Anwendungsaufgaben stellt, z. B. ein Wort nachschlagen lassen und die *headwords* auf der entsprechenden Seite benennen.

Aufgabe 3:

Die SuS üben das Nachschlagen. Sie übersetzen die Ländernamen, kontrollieren mithilfe eines Wörterbuchs und schlagen die Nationalitäten nach.

Lösungen

Aufgabe 1:

a) gratitude – gravel – grave yard – gravity– grayish – greasy spoon – greedy – green

b) slight – slim – sling - slink – slip– slit – slither – sliver

c) icing – icon – idea – idealize – identical – identify – ideogram – idle

d) paternal – path – pathetic – patience – patisserie – patriot – pattern – paucity

Aufgabe 2:

a) physiotherapist, pianissimo, picker, picnic

b) fragment, fragrance, frailty, franchise, freak

Aufgabe 3:

German	English country	Englisch nationality
Sambia	Zambia	Zambian
Namibia	Namibia	Namibian
Kroatien	Croatia	Croatian
Slowenien	Slovenia	Slovenian
Nicaragua	Nicaragua	Nicaraguan
Norwegen	Norway	Norwegian
Island	Iceland	Icelandic
Vietnam	Vietnam	Vietnamese

Worksheet 33: Dictionary skills: A bike

Lernziel

Umgang mit dem Wörterbuch trainieren

Material

Wörterbücher

Kommentar

Anhand des Wortfeldes Fahrrad üben die SuS das Nachschlagen von Wörtern.

Aufgabe 1:

Die SuS suchen die vorgegebenen deutschen Wörter und schreiben sie an das Bild.

Aufgabe 2:

Die SuS lesen die Umschreibungen und erkennen das passende Wort aus Aufgabe 1. Dies kann in Einzel- oder Partnerarbeit geschehen. Leistungsstarke SuS können weitere Wörter paraphrasieren und andere raten lassen.

Aufgabe 3:

Die SuS wenden im Rahmen der kreativen Schreibaufgabe die Wörter aus Aufgabe 1 an. In Einzelarbeit erstellen sie einen Text.

Extra:

Die Aufgaben A-C bieten drei Ansätze zum kreativen Schreiben.

Lösungen

Aufgabe 1:

a) *Gangschaltung:* gears – *Lenker:* handlebars – *Vorderlicht:* front light – *Bremse:* brake – *Federung:* suspension – *Reifen:* tyre – *Rahmen:* frame – *Pedal:* pedal – *Kette:* chain – *Ventil:* valve – *Rücklicht:* rear light – *Schutzblech:* mudguard (AE: mudflap, fender) – *Sattel:* saddle – *Gepäckträger:* rack, carrier

b) individuelle Lösungen, z. B. *Schloss*: lock – *Flickzeug*: repair kit – *Luftpumpe*: bycicle tyre inflator, air pump – *Klingel*: bell – *Reflektor*: reflector – *Griff*: bar end – *Speiche*: spoke – *Flaschenhalter* – bottle cage

Aufgabe 2:

1. saddle
2. handlebars
3. rack, carrier
4. valve
5. front light, rear light, lights, reflectors
6. gear lever

Kommentar mit Lösungen

Worksheet 34: An Australia quiz

Lernziele

- Landeskundliche Informationen zu Australien kennen lernen
- Leseverständnis trainieren

Kommentar

Aufgabe 1:

In Aufgabe 1 lesen die SuS in Partnerarbeit die Quizfragen über Australien und entscheiden, ob diese richtig oder falsch sind. In der Entscheidungsphase sollen sie einander ihren Entschluss begründen.

Lösungen

1. right, 2. right, 3. right, 4. wrong, 5. right, 6. right, 7. wrong, 8. wrong, 9. right, 10. right, 11. wrong, 12. right, 13. right, 14. right

Worksheet 35: The Simpson Desert Bike Challenge

Lernziele

- Textverständnis mithilfe des reziproken Lesens erlangen
- Landeskundliche Informationen zu Australien kennen lernen

Material

Wörterbücher, pro Gruppe ein Set Rollenkärtchen mit den Leseaufträgen (**WS 35.2**)

Kommentar

Die Texterschließung erfolgt mithilfe des reziproken Lesens, einer Form des kooperativen Lernens basierend auf den Überlegungen Norm Greens, Ludger Brüning und Tobias Saum, bei dem sich Phasen der Einzelarbeit mit Phasen der Gruppenarbeit abwechseln.
Die Klasse teilt sich in Gruppen zu je vier SuS, die in rotierender Folge verschiedene Rollen im Leseprozess übernehmen. Es ist hilfreich, wenn LuL dazu für jede Gruppe ein Set Kärtchen (s. unten) vorbereitet hat (**WS 35.2**), auf denen die Aufgaben stehen und die dann weitergereicht werden können, sodass den SuS immer klar ist, welche Rolle sie jeweils gerade haben.

A	B	C	D
Ask your group members questions that can be answered after reading the paragraph.	Give a summary of the paragraph. Your group members will tell you if it was well done. If not, they will correct wrong facts or add information.	Search for unknown words and phrases and explain them to your group.	Predict what is going to happen in the next paragraph.

Alle SuS erhalten den Lesetext und ihr Rollenkärtchen, dann lesen sie in Einzelarbeit den ersten Abschnitt. Sind alle damit fertig, beginnt die Gruppenarbeitsphase.

A stellt Fragen an die Gruppenmitglieder, die aus dem Text heraus beantwortet werden können.
B formuliert eine Zusammenfassung des Abschnitts, die Gruppenmitglieder überlegen, ob diese gelungen ist, korrigieren und/oder ergänzen.
C erklärt unbekannte Wörter und Wendungen mithilfe des Wörterbuchs. Verständnislücken werden im Gespräch mit der Gruppe geschlossen.
D trifft eine Vorhersage, was der nächste Abschnitt bringen wird. Beim letzten Abschnitt kann er/sie einem anderen SuS helfen. Beim Lesen des zweiten Abschnitts und aller folgenden werden die Rollen im Uhrzeigersinn getauscht.

Ludger Brüning, Tobias Saum: Erfolgreich unterrichten durch kooperatives Lernen, Verlagsgesellschaft Neue Deutsche Schule, 2008.

Extra:

Im Anschluss an die intensive Lesephase können die SuS eine kreative Schreibaufgabe wählen.

Worksheet 36: Virtual water

Lernziele

- Lesekompetenz trainieren
- Umgang mit Wasser überdenken

Material

Wörterbücher

Kommentar

Es ist den SuS überlassen, ob sie allein oder mit einem Partner arbeiten. Die SuS lesen den Text über virtuelles Wasser und bearbeiten im Anschluss die Aufgaben dazu.

Aufgabe 1:

Mithilfe der Fragen und der Mindmap erschließen die SuS den Text vertiefend.

Aufgabe 2:

Die SuS machen sich bewusst, wie viel Wasser in den genannten Dingen „versteckt" enthalten ist. Bei dieser Aufgabe muss geraten werden. Die Zahl 140l ist im Lesetext im Bezug auf Kaffee erwähnt. Der tägliche Wasserverbrauch eines Deutschen lässt sich anhand der Angabe im Text errechnen (1,545 m³ entsprechen 1.545.000 Litern geteilt durch 365 Tage). Im Plenum sollte aber im Anschluss an die Bearbeitung der Aufgaben die richtige Lösung preisgegeben werden. Außerdem sollte unbedingt über das Phänomen *virtual water* gesprochen werden, um die SuS für ihre Umwelt zu sensibilisieren. Dazu bietet auch die **Extra**-Aufgabe Gelegenheit. Hier können die SuS diskutieren, z. B. ob sie auf Fleisch verzichten oder Tee statt Kaffee trinken oder mit weniger T-Shirts auskommen würden.

Lösungen

a) 1. true, 2. false

b) mögliche Lösungen zu *virtual water*: growing plants, processing goods, water footprint, water resources, high water consuming products, cubic metre, litre, ml, water depletion, water quality

2. A German needs **4,200 l** of virtual water every day.
A cup of coffee contains **140 l** of virtual water, a cup of tea **35 l**,
2,700 l are needed for a cotton T-shirt, **15,500 l** for 1 kg of beef.
There are **10 l** in a A4 sheet of paper and **13 l** in a 70 g tomato.

Worksheet 37: Spice it up!

Lernziele

- Lesekompetenz trainieren
- Schlüsselwörter finden
- fremde Gewürze kennen lernen
- Rezepte/Instruktionen lesen und verstehen

Material – optional

- Wenn vorhanden, Gewürze zum Riechen mitbringen
- Kärtchen für das Living Memory (s. Warm-up)
- ggf. Zutaten für Lassi
- ggf. Schere

Kommentar

Wenn möglich, geben LuL zu Stundenbeginn kleine Döschen mit jeweils einem Gewürz darin durch die Klasse. Die SuS verankern die unbekannten Namen der Gewürze so multisensorisch. Um Neugier auf Fremdes zu wecken, wurden hier bewusst eher unbekannte Gewürze gewählt.

Kommentar mit Lösungen

Spielerisches Warm-up:

Zur Einführung der neuen Vokabeln spielen die SuS Living Memory. Dazu schreiben LuL im Vorfeld die Gewürze auf einzelne Kärtchen. Jedes Gewürz muss doppelt vorhanden sein. 16 SuS ziehen jeweils ein Kärtchen, lesen das geheime Wort still und „sind" nun das Gewürz. Sie stellen sich auf einen Platz innerhalb des „Spielfeldes" (freier Raum im Klassenzimmer) und bewegen sich nicht von der Stelle. Wie bei einem klassischen Memory-Spiel befragen die verbleibenden zwei oder drei SuS abwechselnd je zwei Mitschüler: *„What spice are you?"* – Antwort beispielsweise: *„I'm lemongrass."* usw. Findet der Fragende ein Paar, darf er weiter raten. Wenn nicht, rät der nächste aus dem Frageteam. Die gefunden Paare setzen sich auf den Boden. LuL oder ein SuS führt an der Tafel eine Strichliste mit den gefundenen Pärchen pro Spieler. Gewonnen hat, wer die meisten Paare gefunden hat. Die SuS sollten dazu angehalten werden, die Frage korrekt zu formulieren und im Satz zu antworten.

Aufgabe 1:

Nun lesen die SuS die Texte über die Gewürze (**WS 37.1**) und füllen die Tabelle (**WS 37.2**) aus. Wenn möglich sollte ohne Wörterbuch gearbeitet werden. Es ist wichtig, sich an Texte zu wagen und deren Inhalt zu verstehen, ohne jedes einzelne Wort zu kennen. In den Lösungen sind alle zu findenden Angaben enthalten. Es kann hier nach Leistungsstand differenziert werden. Lernschwächere SuS suchen nach Angaben zu *taste, smell, colour* oder s*hape*, lernstärkere SuS ergänzen darüber hinaus die Nutzung und Wirkung der Gewürze.

Aufgabe 2:

Die SuS lesen die durcheinander gemischten Rezepte, ordnen zu und nummerieren. Ggf. können die SuS auch die Textabschnitte ausschneiden, um sie dem jeweiligen Gericht in der richtigen Reihenfolge zuzuordnen. Sind in der Schule die Möglichkeiten gegeben, das Lassi-Rezept tatsächlich auszuprobieren, so sollten die SuS dies unbedingt tun.

Lösungen
Aufgabe 1:

no.	spice	region	taste – smell – colour - shape
1	lemongrass	South East Asia	used for marinating fish, chicken or meat, as tea it is refreshing and works against a lack of concentration, green, like fresh lemon
2	fenugreek	India	used in chutneys and sauces, keeps fever low, treatment for diabetes, high blood pressure and stomach aches, bitter, like burnt sugar, brown seeds
3	cinnamon	Indonesia	used in desserts and pastries and in teas, stimulates the blood circulation, good against colds, brown, bark, sweet, pungent, fragrant
4	kurkuma	Africa / India	used in curries because of the deeply yellow colour, nearly tasteless, antiseptic and antibiotic function, part of a root
5	chili	South America	rich in Vitamin C, promotes digestion, can be pain-relievinggreen or red, like small bell peppers, incredibly hot and pungent
6	cardamom	Turkey / India	used as aroma in curries and chais (Indian milk teas), promotes digestion, makes a fresh breath, green, black and white
7	poppy seed	India	used in cakes and pastries and to thicken curries, consists of white or black seeds, aromatic, nutty
8	star anise	Asia	popular taste in drinks and confections, soothes the stomach, stimulates digestion, looks like a star, bitter-sweet, liquorice-like

Kommentar mit Lösungen

Aufgabe 2:

A 2 – B 3 – A 1 – A 4 – A 3 – B 2 – B 1

A. Lassi – a typical Indian drink

A. 1   The beverage consists of fresh fruit and milk or yoghurt. Essential for lassi drinks are the spices that are added. Try this recipe:
A. 2   You need 250 g yoghurt, 100 ml water, 150 g mango (cut into small pieces), 4 teaspoons sugar, 1 teaspoon lemon juice, some rose water, a pinch of cardamom.
A. 3   Put the mango in a mixer and blend well with yoghurt and water.
A. 4   Put in all the other ingredients and stir well. Decorate with daisies, mint or balm leaves.

B. Indian chicken

B.1   You need 3 chicken breasts, cut into small pieces and salted, 5 tablespoons oil, 1 tablespoon butter, 1½ tablespoons cardamom, 1 tablespoon chili, 1 tablespoon kurkuma, 2 tablespoons canned tomatoes, 300 g yoghurt, 300 ml water, salt.
B.2   Heat up oil and butter, put in cardamom then add the chicken breast and deep fry. Put in the other spices and tomatoes. Stir well.
B.3   Put in the yoghurt and add the water gradually. Cook for about 15 minutes. Serve with rice.

Worksheet 38: Being polite

Lernziele

- Lesekompetenz trainieren
- Sich interkulturelle Kompetenz und Höflichkeitsformen aneignen

Kommentar

Aufgabe 1:

a) Die SuS bearbeiten den Fragenbogen in Einzelarbeit.

b) Anschließend diskutieren sie den Fragebogen in Partnerarbeit. Sie begründen sich gegenseitig ihre Entscheidungen und beziehen die Einschätzung des Partners ein, ggf. ändern sie daraufhin ihre Antwort.
Im Plenum kann ebenfalls über die Fragen diskutiert werden.

Extra:

Bei diesen Aufgaben können die SuS selbst Situationen beschreiben, in denen es auf das persönliche Verhalten besonders ankommt.

Lösungen

1b, 2c, 3b, 4c, 5a, 6c, 7a, 8c

Worksheet 39: Let's talk: On a class trip

Lernziel

Schulung der kommunikativen Kompetenzen

Kommentar

WS 39.1 – 39.5 bietet fünf mal zwei *role cards* mit kommunikativen Situationen die mit dem Kontext einer Klassenfahrt durchaus der Lebenswirklichkeit der SuS entsprechen. Die SuS suchen sich eine der Situationen aus und erarbeiten mithilfe der Vorgaben paarweise die Dialoge. In **WS 39.5** übernimmt ein SuS zwei Rollen (Schwester und Arzt), indem er/sie Körperhaltung, Gestik und Standort ändert, sodass klar ist, dass nun eine andere Person dargestellt wird. Da nicht alle SuS alle Worksheets gleichzeitig brauchen, kann die Anzahl der Kopien niedrig gehalten werden.
Die Realisierung der Kommunikationsabsicht ist hier wichtiger als Fehlerfreiheit. Den SuS soll bewusst werden, dass es immer mehrere Varianten gibt, einen Gedanken auszudrücken. Für eine zielorientierte Kommunikation ist es in erster Linie wichtig, dass ihr Gegenüber sie verstehen kann – dazu können sie auch ganz einfache Sätze formulieren. Es sollte ausreichend Zeit bleiben zum Vorstellen der Dialoge, wenn möglich sollten diese gespielt werden.

Kommentar mit Lösungen

Worksheet 40: Food words: A guessing game
Worksheet 41: Sport words: A guessing game

Lernziele

- Kommunikative Kompetenz trainieren
- Wortschatz food bzw. sport trainieren

Material

Stoppuhr

Kommentar

Um den SuS die Spielidee zu verdeutlichen, bekommt jede/r SuS ein Kärtchen aus dem Spielset. Zwei SuS sitzen sich gegenüber und erklären die Begriffe auf der Karte.
Das Gegenüber muss die Begriffe erraten. In leistungsstarken Klassen kann dieser Schritt wegfallen.

LuL erklärt die Spielregeln und hält diese ggf. an der Tafel oder auf Folie per OHP für alle gut lesbar fest.

Rules:

- Two teams play against each other. Each team takes turns sending two players (A and B) to the front.
- The players sit facing each other.
- Player A chooses a category for the words he/she is going to explain.
- The players have got one minute to explain and guess the words.
- When explaining a word player A is not allowed to – use his/her hands (the player can sit on his/her hands) – use German words – use parts of the words – say "It starts with the letter …"

Spielvorbereitung:
In einem Raster/einer Tabelle notiert LuL die verschiedenen Kategorien (linke Spalte der Spielkarten – siehe Kopiervorlage) als Tafelanschrieb oder auf Folie.

Spielablauf:
Die Klasse wird in zwei Teams geteilt. Jedes Team schickt abwechselnd zwei Spieler nach vorn. Spieler A sucht sich eine Kategorie von der Tafel aus. Der Spielleiter (LuL/SuS) gibt die entsprechende Karte heraus und achtet darauf, dass nur Spieler A die Wörter auf der Rückseite erkennt. Der Spielleiter achtet auf die Zeit und darauf, dass die Regeln eingehalten werden. Pro erratenes Wort gibt es einen Punkt für das jeweilige Team. Der Punktestand wird an der Tafel festgehalten. Das Team mit den meisten Punkten gewinnt.

Worksheet 42: Jobtivity

Lernziele

- Kommunikative Kompetenz trainieren
- Wortfeld Berufe festigen

Material

- Würfel, Spielfiguren (z. B. Münzen)
- Stoppuhr

Kommentar

Dieses Spiel ist eine auf das Wortfeld jobs abgewandelte Variante des Spieleklassikers Activity.
Die Klasse teilt sich in Teams zu drei oder vier SuS. Um ein Startteam zu finden, würfelt jedes Team reihum einmal, das Team mit der höchsten Augenzahl beginnt, danach geht es im Uhrzeigersinn weiter.
Ein SuS des Startteams zieht eine Karte und kann sich für einen darauf stehenden Begriff entscheiden. Das Symbol vor dem Begriff zeigt an, ob dieser erklärt, gezeichnet oder pantomimisch dargestellt werden soll. Die anderen Teammitglieder müssen in einer Minute den Begriff erraten.
Das benachbarte Team darf den Begriff sehen und achtet auf das Einhalten der Zeit. Hat das Team den Begriff erraten, darf es die eigene Spielfigur auf dem Spielplan so viele

92

Felder nach vorn schieben, wie für den Begriff auf der Karte angegeben. Die anderen Teams verfahren ebenso.

Ab der nächsten Runde muss der Begriff genommen werden, der mit dem Symbol auf dem jeweiligen Feld übereinstimmt: Kommt Team A beispielsweise in Runde 1 auf ein Feld mit einem Stift, heißt das, in Runde 2 ist der Begriff, der auf der Karte mit diesem Symbol gekennzeichnet ist, zeichnerisch darzustellen. Das benachbarte Team überprüft auch dies. In sehr großen Klassen kann man zwei Großgruppen mit zwei Spielplänen spielen lassen.

Berufe

bank clerk – *Bankangestellte/r*
beautitian – *Kosmetiker/in*
blacksmith – *Schmied*
bricklayer – *Maurer*
butcher – *Fleischer/Metzger*
carpenter – *Zimmermann*
conductor – *Dirigent/in*
dentist – *Zahnarzt, Zahnärztin*
flight attendant – *Steward, Stewardess*
flight controller – *Fluglotse*
forester – *Förster*
horse breeder – *Pferdezüchter/in*
interpreter – *Dolmetscher/in, Übersetzer/in*
plumber – *Installateur, Klempner*
press officer – *Pressesprecher/in*
receptionist – *Empfangsmitarbeiter/in, Sprechstundenhilfe*
restorer – *Restaurator/in*
roofer – *Dachdecker*
sales representative – *Außendienstmitarbeiter/in, Handelsvertreter/in*
shepherd – *Schäfer*
street sweeper – *Straßenkehrer*
tailor – *Schneider/in*
travel agent – *Reisekaufmann/-frau*
wine-grower – *Winzer/in*
zookeeper – *Tierpfleger/in*

Worksheet 43: Dictionary skills: False friends

Lernziele

- Umgang mit Wörterbuch trainieren
- *False friends* erkennen

Material

Wörterbücher

Kommentar

Aufgabe 1:

Mithilfe des Wörterbuchs übersetzen die SuS in Einzelarbeit die Wörter in den beiden Tabellen. Im Anschluss daran erledigen sie die Multiple-Choice Aufgabe.

Extra:

Diese Aufgabe vermittelt die Arbeit mit Kartei-Karten als Lerntechnik.

Lösungen

Aufgabe 1a:

German	English
Mappe	folder
Eintrittskarte	ticket
aktuell	current, up to date
sympathisch	friendly, likable
Bank	bank; bench
bekommen	get
eventuell	maybe
Unternehmer	employer
Prospekt	brochure, leaflet
ordinär	vulgar
sensibel	sensitive

English	German
map	Land-Karte
(post)card	Grußkarte
actual	tatsächlich, wirklich
sympathetic	mitfühlend
bank	Bank; Ufer
become	werden
eventual	letztendlich, schließlich
undertaker	Bestatter
prospect	Ausblick, Zukunftsaussicht
ordinary	gewöhnlich, durchschnittlich
sensible	sinnvoll, vernünftig

Aufgabe 1b:

1. map, 2. ticket, 3. folder, 4. sensitive, 5. sensible, 6. employer, 7. bench, 8. maybe, 9. sympathetic, 10. get, 11. brochure, leaflet, 12. ordinary

Worksheet 44: Dictionary skills: Synomyms

Lernziel

Wortschatzarbeit: Synonyme verwenden

Material

Wörterbücher

Kommentar

Aufgabe 1:

Die SuS verbinden die passenden Wörter mit Linien zu Paaren. Das Wörterbuch kann dabei benutzt werden.

Aufgabe 2:

Hier ersetzen die SuS das fett gedruckte Wort durch ein Synonym. Dies geschieht in Einzelarbeit. Ist ein SuS fertig, geht er/sie an eine vorher bestimmte Stelle im Raum und wartet dort auf den nächsten.
Die beiden kontrollieren gegenseitig ihre Arbeitsblätter, ggf. diskutieren sie die Lösung. Bei Unklarheiten wenden sie sich an den LuL.

Aufgabe 3:

Die SuS suchen mithilfe des Wörterbuchs die deutsche Übersetzung (englisch-deutsches Wörterbuch) und ein Synonym für das englische Wort (deutsch-englisches Wörterbuch oder Thesaurus).

Lösungen

Aufgabe 1:

angry – furious, difficult – hard, careful – cautious, buy – purchase, leave – depart, close – near, rude – impolite, lucky – fortunate, persuade – convince, surprised – amazed, find – locate

Aufgabe 2:

1. locate, 2. impolite, 3. purchased, 4. difficult, 5. near, 6. cautious, 7. furious, 8. amazed, 9. depart, 10. fortunate, 11. convince

Aufgabe 3:

German	English synonyms	
aufmerksam, rücksichtsvoll	considerate	thoughtful
modern, zeitgemäß	modern	contemporary
engagiert	committed	dedicated
Katastrophe	catastrophe	disaster
jmd ärgern, stören	(to) annoy s.o.	(to) bother s.o.
vertrauenswürdig, zuverlässig	trustworthy	reliable
Dramatiker	playwright	dramatist

Bildquellennachweis

Cover (von links nach rechts) Thinkstock (istockphoto), München – shutterstock (Luciano Mortula) New York, NY – MEV Verlag GmbH, Augsburg – Sandra Vrabec, Stuttgart; **10** shutterstock (AlexKalashnikov), New York, NY; **11** shutterstock (Nik Niklz), New York, NY; **11** Fotolia LLC (Gentoo Multimedia), New York; **14** Getty Images, München; **14** Alamy Images (D Hale-Sutton), Abingdon, Oxon; **31** shutterstock (DFree), New York, NY; **32** Fotolia LLC, New York; **35** Heinzmann, Stefan, Rodewisch; **36** Heinzmann, Stefan, Rodewisch; **37** shutterstock (Suzanne Tucker), New York, NY; **47** iStockphoto (Petre Milevski), Calgary, Alberta; **48** Klett-Archiv (Kreaktor GmbH), Stuttgart; **48** shutterstock (WMJ), New York, NY; **48** iStockphoto (On-Air), Calgary, Alberta; **48** shutterstock (Sergey Mikhaylov), New York, NY; **49** Getty Images (Ezra Shaw), München; **51** shutterstock (nld), New York, NY; **52** Eisermann, Bettina, Rodewisch

Sollte es in einem Einzelfall nicht gelungen sein, den korrekten Rechteinhaber ausfindig zu machen, so werden berechtigte Ansprüche selbstverständlich im Rahmen der üblichen Regelungen abgegolten.